# JAMES SCOTT

RECOLLECTIONS
OF
A NAVAL LIFE

Volume II

Elibron Classics
www.elibron.com

Elibron Classics series.

© 2005 Adamant Media Corporation.

ISBN 1-4021-9828-0 (paperback)
ISBN 1-4212-9906-2 (hardcover)

This Elibron Classics Replica Edition is an unabridged facsimile
of the edition published in 1834 by Richard Bentley,
London.

Elibron and Elibron Classics are trademarks of
Adamant Media Corporation. All rights reserved.

This book is an accurate reproduction of the original. Any marks, names, colophons, imprints, logos or other symbols or identifiers that appear on or in this book, except for those of Adamant Media Corporation and BookSurge, LLC, are used only for historical reference and accuracy and are not meant to designate origin or imply any sponsorship by or license from any third party.

RECOLLECTIONS

OF

A NAVAL LIFE.

BY

CAPTAIN JAMES SCOTT, R.N.

> In life!—we skim the surface of the deep,
> To battle with our country's foes.
> In death!—we sink beneath the curling wave,
> Leaving but a circling eddy
> To proclaim our resting-place, and fate.

IN THREE VOLUMES.

VOL. II.

LONDON:
RICHARD BENTLEY, NEW BURLINGTON STREET,
Publisher in Ordinary to His Majesty.

1834.

LONDON:
PRINTED BY SAMUEL BENTLEY,
Dorset Street, Fleet Street.

CONTENTS

OF

THE SECOND VOLUME.

CHAPTER I.

Despatches from Sheerness. The Surgeon's loss. Arrival at Sheerness with our Prize. Our Royal Visiters. Congratulations of my Family. Capture of La Guerrière by the Americans. Particulars of that event, and reflections relative thereto. Desertions consequent on our mode of Impressment. Severity of American discipline. Rejoin the Blanche. Return to Spithead. Bid farewell to my messmates and friends. Rejoin Captain C. Expedition to Buenos Ayres. An accident. Appointment of incompetent men to our Ships-of-War. Fatal instance of this. Noble presence of mind of Captain Hickey. . . . . . . page 1

CHAPTER II.

Activity of our First Lieutenant. Arrive off the Island of St. Jago. A strange Schooner. Precautions against a suspected danger. Amusement at St. Jago. Hospitality of a Portuguese Peasant. Fishing at Porto Praya. Embarkation of Cannon. Anchor in Fayal Bay. A Dangerous Situation. Return to Portsmouth. Appointed to take charge of the East India Convoy. Interference of the Leadenhall-street Establishment. Difficulties attending the charge of a Convoy. Join Sir S. Hood's Squadron. Peak of Teneriffe. Loss of three men by falling overboard. Reflections. Repair to Madeira. A bill for Breakfast. Diving. A narrow Escape. . . . 31

CHAPTER III.

Placed on board the Achille. Blockade. Master's Mates. A Cock-pit Orpheus. Fracas with the Caterer of the Mess. His complaint to the Captain. Jocular Revenge of the Middies. Consequent partition of the Larboard Berth. Follow-my-Leader. Grampus blowing. 51

CHAPTER IV.

Ordered into Port. Moored in Cawsand Bay. Join Captain C— in the Pompée. My new Messmates. Proceed off Rochfort. Frolic in l'Isle du Rhé. A Guernsey Privateer aground. Exertions to save her. Ordered to perform the duty of a Lieutenant. Reflections on the propriety of accustoming young men to the command of the Deck. My new honours threatened with a speedy termination. An Accident. Inquiry and Acquittal Fall in with a suspicious Schooner. Rejoin the Impetueux. Unexpected present of Wine. A strange Sail. The Chase. The Capture. A Recognition. Sent with Lieutenant M— to take charge of the Prize. The Yellow Fever on board her. Terrible ravage of the disease. I am seized by the contagion. Death of Mr. Booth. The Black Vomit. My convalescence. Yellow Jack. A Presentiment. Reflections. . 63

CHAPTER V.

Cruise in Fort Royal Bay, Martinique. Successful manœuvre of the French Frigate l'Amphitrite. Recapture the Lord Cranston, a letter of marque. The late Mr. Maxwell's hospitalities. A Dignity Ball. Mulatto Beauties. Their coquetry. Nancy Clarke. Attention and kindness of Mulatto Nurses. Negroes at Bridge Town, Barbadoes. An Affray. Danger from fire of a Prize Vessel. Rejoin the Pompée. Interchange of courtesies. Ship cleared for action. A narrow Escape. Captain P–h–ll's action with La Topaze. Melancholy occurrence. Arrival of the Expedition for the attack of Martinique. Pigeon Island reconnoitred. Explosion of a Shell. Difficult formation of a Hill-Battery. Reduction of Pigeon Island. 97

CHAPTER VI.

Lieutenant-General Beckwith's decided action. Take possession of Fort Royal. Erection of Batteries. An Accident. Loss of life during the construction of the Sailors' Battery. Manœuvres to avoid the Shells. Conveying the Guns to the Battery. Mulatto Girls. A dangerous Adventure. Cool and intrepid conduct of Captain S—th of the Engineers. The Batteries completed. The Bombardment. The Enemy's sally repulsed. Merit neglected. A Truce. Hostilities recommenced. The Author wounded. Kindness of his messmates. He is removed on board. Surrender of Fort Bourbon. Author visits the Fort. The captive Garrison embarked. Court Martial on the Officers and Men of the Carnation. The Sentence. Reflections. The Execution. 129

CHAPTER VII.

Quit the Pompée. Reception of the late Governor and suite on board the Belleisle. Bills of Exchange for Prize-money. Departure from Port Royal. Devotion of his Officers to Napoleon. Arrival in Quiberon Bay. Negotiation for Exchange of Prisoners. A Frenchman's Trick. Departure of the French Governor and suite. My anxiety to proceed to London. An unlucky meeting. A Rebuke. Lucky Escape. The expedition to Walcheren. Disembarcation of the Troops. Investment of Flushing. Gallantry of the Raven brig. Force the passage between Cadsand and Flushing. Completion of the Batteries against Flushing. The Bombardment. Surrender of the Town. A French Sergeant's remark. Horrors of War. Freedom of England from its Devastation. Claims of our Defenders on the National Gratitude. 165

CHAPTER VIII.

Treaty for the evacuation of the works of Flushing. Attempt by the Enemy's gun-boats. Our flotilla. The Army moves towards Bathz. An invitation. Unpleasant result. Agreeable surprise. Appointed Lieutenant to the Resolution. Attacked by the malignant fever. Nominated to His Majesty's Ship F—che. Proceed to the Downs. Ordered into harbour. An altercation and Court-Martial. Return home. Appointed to the Myrtle. Captain Napier. Arrive at Lisbon. Turned over to the Barfleur. Ward-room mess of that ship. Scenery about Lisbon. Condition of the city. Approach of the Duke of Wellington towards Lisbon. Superstition. Black Crosses. Frequency of Murder in Lisbon. Arrival of the Myrtle. Captain Cowan. 196

CHAPTER IX.

Trip to Cadiz. The French open a fire on us. Touch at Gibraltar. Proceed to Algiers. Our Jewish friend. A Dispute. Bathing. Fidelity and sagacity of a Newfoundland Dog. Return to Lisbon. A bereaved family. Trial for High Treason. Terrible Execution. 226

CHAPTER X.

Convoy a merchant vessel to Madeira and the Cape de Verd Islands. The Dog and the Turtles. Put into Porto Praya. Slave ships. Send Boats up the Gambia. James's Island. Land-crabs. Horrible resting-place. Fall in with a Goree trader. Enormous Ant-hills. Flamingoes. Capture a Slave Schooner. Traffic in human flesh. Liberation of Slaves. 248

CHAPTER XI.

Remarks on the Slave Question. . . 260

CHAPTER XII.

Rejoin the Myrtle. Precautions to preserve the health of the Ship's Company. March of a body of White Ants. They are molested. Their revenge. Descendants of the Maroons. "General Montague." Fruit at Sierra Leone. A Slave-brig. Tragical Occurrence. A White Negress. A captive boy taken as a Servant. His incorrigible propensity to theft. Parrots. Polly and Blacky. Ordered to the assistance of the Arethusa. Tornadoes. An Accident. A second trip up the Gambia. A Black Trafficker in Slaves. Bivouac on James's Island. Deleterious atmosphere of the Gambia. Arrive at Goree. A Native shipped as a Landsman. Anecdote . 301

RECOLLECTIONS

OF A

NAVAL LIFE.

CHAPTER I.

Despatches from Sheerness—The Surgeon's loss—Arrival at Sheerness with our Prize—Our Royal Visiters—Congratulations of my Family—Capture of La Guerrière by the Americans—Particulars of that event, and reflections relative thereto—Desertions consequent on our mode of Impressment—Severity of American discipline—Rejoin the Blanche—Return to Spithead—Bid farewell to my messmates and friends—Rejoin Captain C.—Expedition to Buenos Ayres—An accident—Appointment of incompetent men to our Ships-of-War—Fatal instance of this—Noble presence of mind of Captain Hickey.

THE return of post brought despatches ordering us to Sheerness to repair our damages. On passing up Swin, we recognized on board a Scotch smack our ill-starred surgeon, who had been left behind at Yarmouth. He had hurried off to London, whence the Admiralty had ordered him to Leith, to await our return. The mortification he experienced on meeting the victorious ship ushering in La Guerrière, may be divined; loss of professional credit and a pretty amount of cash was sufficiently stunning to this hapless disciple of Galen: such a misfortune must be felt in all its poignancy when the monitor within tells us that we have been the architect of our own disappointment, by listening to the dictates, or administering too freely to the indulgence, of any engrossing passion.

On arriving at Sheerness, the prize was ordered up to Chatham, our vacillating *ci-devant* pilot taking charge of her. We had not rounded the first point of the reach before he succeeded in runing us ashore, and there we were planted until the following tide; but by lightening the ship of her guns, we succeeded in getting off without sustaining any very material damage. As the prize passed the French prisoners in the hulks, we were assailed with a smart volley of groans, hissing, howlings, and *sacres*: we afterwards learned that these revilings were intended for their partners in misfortune, the trim appearance of La Guerrière having created the painful suspicion that she had prematurely struck her colours. Had they immediately after the action seen the dismantled condition of the Blanche, and the shattered hull of the prize, their wounded feelings would perhaps have found some relief.

The work of dismantling the prize preparatory to delivering her over to the officers of the dockyard, went on rapidly. While thus employed, a grand review of all the troops in the environs of Chatham, by His Royal Highness the Duke of York, took place on the ground immediately overlooking that part of the river where we were lying. About noon the mimic fight ceased. We had piped to dinner, the officers had descended to their luncheon, and I was left alone walking the deck, ruminating on the pleasure and congratulations that were awaiting me at home, when I was startled from my reverie by a voice from alongside, "I'll thank you for a rope — a rope:"— hurrying to the gangway, and looking over the side, I beheld a barge full of military officers, glittering in their gorgeous suits of scarlet and gold. One of the party addressed me, "We will thank you for a rope, young gentleman." Regardless of their white gloves, I immediately threw over the only side ropes at hand, and scampered down to our commanding officer to report the unexpected arrival of a boat load of red-coats. On returning to the deck, I found, to my astonishment, already mounted on the gangway—His Royal Highness the Duke of York, who was immediately followed by the Dukes of Cumberland and Cambridge, escorted by Earl Moira, and a numerous suite of general officers. We were completely taken aback, and not a little vexed that we should be found deficient in those external marks of honour and etiquette due to the illustrious visiters. The feelings of Lieutenant D—s were quickly perceived, and his apologies cut short by that *suaviter in modo*, the peculiar and ingratiating gift of the Royal family, accompanied by a polite desire to be conducted round the ship. On descending to the main-deck, His Royal Highness appeared much struck with the mischief we had committed. "Very pretty shot indeed!"—"Capital! that must have been a wicked messenger," pointing to traces of blood that by some oversight still remained too visible on the beams and deck overhead—" Hot work for the poor Frenchmen!" were the occasional remarks that broke from the Duke, as he moved along the decks. After visiting every part of the vessel, His Royal Highness entered into conversation with the officers, inquiring into the progress of our career in the service, and the captains we had served under, adding to the two Middies, " It is a pity you have not served your time; I hope you will have many more claims to swell the amount of those you can now bring forward." Our Royal visiters departed apparently much gratified, leaving us in a high state of delight at the unexpected honour they had conferred upon us.

Captain Lavie proceeded to London, and received the honour of knighthood; the first lieutenant obtained the epaulette; the warrant officers were promoted to line-of-battle ships, and some of the best men got warrants. Not one Middy had served his time, therefore we remained *in statu quo.* During the period of dismantling, I was overjoyed at receiving a visit from my father, who could not resist the temptation of posting from London to share in the triumphant feelings of his son. I had the pleasure of conducting him round the ship, and have never felt a purer enjoyment than that day afforded me. As the prize was not ready for delivering over to the charge of the dock-yard, I was unable to accompany the old gentleman home; but a few days of hard work allowed me afterwards to enjoy the congratulations of my family and friends. A pile of the most tempting invitations awaited my arrival; had my sojourn been six weeks instead of six days, I could not have availed myself of all the flattering attentions that were showered upon me: of course the whole battle was fought over and over again, till I was in a promising way of being surfeited with the oft-repeated tale, and I positively welcomed the day that placed me *en route* for my ship.

I gave a parting benediction to La Guerrière as I passed her in the Sheerness boat, little contemplating that she, who had gained us so pretty a share of credit, would be the first ship to fall into the power of the United States of America.

Notwithstanding the inequality of the contest, it was doubtless a severe blow to the pride of the

British navy to behold one vessel after another falling into the enemy's hands.* I am inclined, however, to believe that their capture has given a

* The force of the Constitution has been already given in the first volume, p. 61. In her action with La Guerrière, she had 460 men on board, the latter only 244. La Guerrière and Java were equal in size and metal. The British loss amounted to 15 killed and 63 wounded, total 78. In Captain Hull's despatch, he makes our loss 101, in which is included 24 missing. The American captain thus accounts for his statement:—" Missing, Lieutenants Pullman and Roberts, and 22 seamen, supposed to have gone overboard with the masts."—Vide *Brennan's* [American] *Naval and Military Letters*, p. 51. These officers and men had been sent away in prizes, which fact Captain Hull ought to have known, by a reference to La Guerrière's log and muster-books, had he not felt satisfied with Captain Dacres's word to that effect. In the American official despatches relative to the capture of our frigates, the respective force of the contending parties is not mentioned, which of course leaves the public in the dark as to the actual merits of the capture. I subjoin an American description of the respective sizes of the Macedonian and United States, after the action which ended in the capture of the former:—

AMERICAN ACCOUNT.

	" *United States.*	*Macedonian.*
" Length	176 feet	166 feet.
Breadth	48	48 ft. 8in.
Tons	1405	1325."

Nile's Register, Vol. IV.

The American frigates, President, United States, and Constitution, did not differ one ton in size from each other, as is shown by the American Government's official accounts; the armament alone varied; the two former carrying 42-pounder carronades most beneficial lesson to the navy, and one which we are bound to remember for years to come. A forcible demonstration of a very sensible piece of

on their upper decks, which the Constitution had changed for 32-pounders, previously to her falling in with La Guerrière. As the President was conducted into Portsmouth harbour by Captain Henry Hope, of the Endymion, our naval architects had ample leisure to measure and re-measure her. No mistake could arise here. In the American comparison, it will be observed that they judiciously keep the principal items of the opponents out of view, viz. *guns and men*. They only modestly add near two hundred and fifty tons to the size of the British frigate, and subtract one hundred and thirty from their own.

TRUE ACCOUNT.

	United States.	Macedonian.
" Broadside guns {	28 n°.	24
	864 lbs.	528
Crew	474	254
Tons	1533	1081."

James's Naval History, Vol. VI.

It appears that the national legislature of America, in awarding its vote of thanks to Commodore Decatur and his crew (with a gold medal to the former, and silver medals to his officers), termed it "the brilliant victory gained by the frigate United States over the British frigate Macedonian." A special committee of the same wise men determined the Macedonian to be equal to the United States. To enhance the merit of the captors, the account in the fourth volume of *Nile's Register* states, that the 24lb. shot of the American frigate weighed only 22lbs.; having made the Java's 18-pounders weigh 21 lbs. They cleverly apply the same additional weight to the Macedonian's 18-pounders: thus the American 24lb. balls are made to approximate within one pound to the English 18-pounders.

advice, which cannot be too strongly engraven upon the minds of commanding officers, has disagreeably intruded itself—" However weak your enemy may be, never despise him."

" It has often happened that a despised enemy has given a bloody battle; and the most renowned kings and nations have been overthrown by a small force."

The Americans deserve every possible credit for the line of conduct they adopted respecting the arrangement and disposal of their squadron; no policy could have been better suited to the circumstances under which they were placed, or more likely to be detrimental to the interest of the nation whose fall they hoped to assist in by coalescing with the French Emperor. They had wisely prepared for the contest by building frigates of such an enormous size and calibre as would with common prudence and courage ensure them a preponderating power over any force of the same denomination they were likely to encounter; and instead of sending their whole squadron to cruise together, they prudently despatched them to different quarters; calculating upon the many chances that existed of falling in with our detached frigates, and the multiplied opportunities of wounding our commercial marine which this dispersion of their vessels gave them.

I have already stated the superiority of the American frigates over the English in size, guns, and the number of their men: this was of course well known to us, but we were not aware of the judicious attention they had paid to render their men perfect in the management of their great guns.

The many sights invented for our marine artillery of late years are doubtless great improvements, and reflect the highest praise upon the different inventors; but the simple one adopted by the Americans appearing to me so advantageous, it has often struck me as wonderful that a maritime nation like ourselves should not have thought of applying something of the kind to our guns throughout the service. The Americans disparted their guns by a piece of deal board of one inch and a quarter in thickness, laid edgewise from the touch-hole to the muzzle, firmly lashed to the piece of ordnance: on the upper edge of the board a groove ran along the centre, (corresponding with the centre line of the piece,) in which were inserted small iron arches to carry the sight forward with greater accuracy. The superior part of the board being formed parallel to the axis of the concave cylinder of the gun, at once afforded the power of pointing their artillery with the nicest exactitude for point-blank distance. But after all said and done upon the subject, there is nothing like following Nelson's mode, when it is practicable, of getting so close to your enemy that you cannot miss him.

A long career of success had engendered the false feeling of security that nothing was able to withstand our arms, and that the mere sight of an English frigate was quite enough to lower the pride of any single-decked vessel that ever swam on the seas. This faulty opinion unfortunately increased in growth towards the Americans, in consequence of the rencontre of the Leopard with the Chesapeake, and the slight resistance offered by the latter; but more particularly from the affair between the President, one of the largest of their frigates, and the Little Belt, sloop-of-war, which made an intrepid but of course useless defence against the cowardly attack of Commodore Rodgers. His greatest feather during the war was, in fact, allowing the Belvidera, a thirty-six gun frigate, to get away from himself and the whole American squadron, after receiving from her a dose which the doughty Commodore so little relished, that he was induced to decline pushing alongside, preferring rather to yaw, giving one broadside and then the other, and allowing his gallant opponent by this means to escape. Had any other officer in the American navy commanded, the probability is, that nothing could have saved Captain Byron and his gallant crew from capture. This brilliant success of the Belvidera added to the feelings of superiority, and in an equal ratio decreased our respect towards the enemy.

The stoppage of American commerce, arising from a state of hostilities and the previous embargo, threw an immense body of their seamen out of employment. The American navy was comparatively small, and in manning their ships they had the option of selecting the best seamen :

among whom, I feel shame as a Briton to confess, were many Englishmen!

Our mode of impressment induced many of these deluded men to proceed to America for the purpose of procuring protections, which they were enabled to obtain with ease. For instance, an English sailor wished for a protection as an American citizen: the candidate for this honour was placed by his friends in a cradle, and the ceremony of rocking him was witnessed by a man old enough to be the aspirant's father; the next day the parties appeared before a magistrate.

"Are you an American-born citizen?"

"I am."

"Is there any inhabitant of this city can identify you as such?"

"There is;"—and the old man who had seen him only the day previously, was brought forward, and swore point-blank that he had seen him rocked in his cradle. This was sufficient, and without further investigation the protection was handed over to the applicant.

Thus were the services of the sons of our own soil brought into play against us, the greater number of whom had been inured to the bloody combat. The advantage of a few veterans to the American Government was incalculable, and they wisely availed themselves of it. These veterans had been led away by a shadow, instead of abiding by the substance. The captivating sounds of liberty and equality, so disinterestedly professed on the Western side of the Atlantic, have led astray many a clearer head and sounder judgment than falls to the lot of poor Jack; we cannot then be surprised that upon such minds the land of freedom and plenty should appear clothed with a thousand charms, particularly for those who had been accustomed to the regular and strict discipline absolutely necessary in a man-of-war. Deprived of employment in the mercantile marine, it needed no great persuasion to induce Jack to enter into the American Government-vessels, where doubtless he expected to cut a prominent figure in the pleasing picture which he had drawn to himself of liberty and equality, differing totally in his own expectation from the course of discipline pursued in the ships belonging to his native land. Yet some of these men, who had entered the

American navy previously to the war, were bold in principle and stout at heart, and firmly refused to serve in arms against their countrymen. In order to deter the less scrupulous portion of their compatriots from following this honourable example, these resolute seamen were tarred, feathered, and then sent on shore, exposed to the ridicule and ill treatment of the mob. So much for the republican liberality of that day; and for the respect they paid to the *amor patriæ* exhibited by these poor fellows!

I have reason to believe that the greater part of the misguided men who remained in the American service bitterly repented the rash step they had taken. It required no long period to elapse after putting to sea, before they found out that "a man may jump out of the frying-pan into the fire." The discipline on board an American man of-war would startle our philanthropists from their propriety, were they to compare it with our own: it is infinitely more severe, and every officer, from the first lieutenant downwards, has the power of inflicting the punishment of flogging with the colt; and this unlimited mode of chastisement takes place in ships belonging to a country where the outcry for the rights of man may be heard ascending in every scale of the gammut!

The Americans are a shrewd, clever people, and quickly discover the path that is likely to terminate most beneficially for their interests; they are too sagacious to allow even the phantom idol of their worship to interfere with or palsy the regulations they may enact for the general welfare, and therefore they permit on board their ships of war a system totally incompatible with their own constitution, and their own cherished ideas of republican freedom. They are properly sensible of the due importance of the authority and discretionary power delegated by the Government to the commanders of their ships of war, and *calculate* correctly upon the advantages and protection that a well-maintained course of naval discipline must ensure to their country.

I wish the advocates of the no-punishment system would have the sense to make themselves masters of this important subject in all its bearings; I cannot admit their competency to judge of the expediency or inexpediency of corporal punishment, until they can produce demonstrative proof of the practicability of their Quixotic speculation on this matter.

Let a couple of dozen of these benevolent gentlemen be placed on board a like number of his Majesty's ships for three years. Possessing by means of this experiment a thorough knowledge of the peculiarities and faults of the crew, the situation of the captain, and the momentous responsibility that the charge of a ship involves, they would be sufficiently prepared for argument, and in every way authorized to pronounce upon so critical a point. I am quite sure that four-and-twenty of the most strenuous of the abolition junta (if their zeal equal their protestations,) would not hesitate to devote themselves to the final settlement of a question which in its present state can only serve to irritate the mind of the sailor, and harass the country at large, encompassing, as it does, the sanity of the root and heart of British power.

Yes: these gentlemen will pause ere they lay the keen edge of the axe to the life-seat of the gallant tree that has for ages defied the beating storm and howling tempest, spreading its gigantic branches to protect the children of the soil that nourishes it from scathe or blight.

Having rejoined the Blanche, refitted, and made good our damages, we repaired to Portsmouth, and from thence to cruise in the Bay of Biscay. An American, of whom we had received correct information, was captured with enemy's property on board and sent in. Here our good luck deserted us; for, the prize meeting with foul weather and losing all her sails, Lieutenant B—, who had charge of her, to avoid a worse fate, found himself under the necessity of bearing up for an enemy's port in Spain, and surrendering himself and crew as prisoners of war.

In company with Rear-Admiral Louis's squadron, the French frigate Presidente was captured, and after a four months' cruise the Blanche returned to Spithead. I here bade an affectionate farewell to my messmates and friends, and rejoined Captain C—, who had then the command of the Captain, seventy-four. Ten days after my last visit to the once fortunate Blanche, she was wrecked on the coast of France!—many lost their lives, and the rest of the crew remained in a French prison till the formidable power of Napoleon was broken, which happily restored them to their native land.

The regret I felt on parting with my late pleasant messmates was in a great measure counterbalanced by the satisfaction I experienced in being again placed under the command of my former captain. The ship I had now joined could not but recall the gallant deeds of Nelson while in the command of her on the glorious 14th of February, when the lofty San Josef, of one hundred and twelve guns, and the San Nicolas, eighty-four, yielded to the superior prowess of the heroic Commodore and his daring band of followers.

We were quickly ordered round to Falmouth, where the expedition to Buenos Ayres was assembled, under the orders of Captain Stopford, in the Spencer. In a few days, in company with the Theseus, Ganges, Nereide, and the Commodore, we took our departure. Our station was that of whipper-in of the convoy, and we accordingly took our position in the rear of the fleet. The officer of the first watch was a young lieutenant of a noble family, who had just joined us.

The Captain remained upon deck till past four bells, and left the ship in that situation with respect to the fleet, (about a mile astern of the convoy,) which he particularly directed might be maintained during the night, accompanied by the usual written night orders relative to any change of circumstance, &c. The wind being right aft, any one would have supposed that it would have been impossible to have erred; but scarcely had the Captain left the deck when the wind freshened, and, no reduction of sail being made, it naturally enough sent us flying ahead: in a very short time we had passed the sternmost vessel, and, to the great dismay of the officer of the watch, he found himself in the thick of the convoy. Had he immediately made known his awkward predicament to the first lieutenant, or had he paid attention to the orders of the night in reporting the circumstance to the Captain, the error would have been speedily rectified; but, unfortunately, pride interfered to prevent this salutary step, and poor B—e's confusion increased with his difficulties. After making many of the smaller craft around us sheer off in dismay at our rapid approach, we got so completely hemmed in on all sides, that to yaw either to port or starboard would have infallibly sent us on board one or the other of them. Still it never struck him to shorten sail, and, in the height of his mismanagement, an extra puff of wind gave the old ship such an impetus that she fairly ran away with him, nor was her speed at all diminished till she dashed rudely upon the slumbers of the astonished soldiers by running stem on, to the stern of one of the finest and largest transports in the fleet. The crash was terrible for the lesser vessel, and must have powerfully shaken the nerves of all the officers' ladies on board; away went her mizen-mast over the side, and in the twinkling of an eye she was a complete wreck.

The instant appearance of the Captain and first Lieutenant prevented further mischief; but when all had been done that could be arranged for the crippled vessel, by taking her in tow and despatching the requisite assistance on board, the unfortunate Lieutenant came in for a lecture that I should have been sorry to have taken upon my own shoulders for a thousand pounds. He had it as hot as he could sup it. It was the first and last time he was permitted to have charge of the ship. I will answer for it, he never saw a transport afterwards, which did not revive the remembrance of the stinging rebuke he that night received. Poor fellow! when he was in command of a sloop of war some years afterwards, she foundered in the Channel, and every soul perished.

It was a melancholy circumstance, and however much I may regret the introduction of the subject, I cannot, in justice to my meritorious brother officers and sympathising countrymen, pass over the palpable share of blame to be attached in this instance to one party, and the lamentable effects resulting from it to another, without strongly animadverting upon the cruelty and irreparable injury done to the service, and to the nation, by the appointment of incompetent men to our ships of war. My unfortunate friend doubtless fell a victim, not only to his utter ignorance of nautical affairs, but to the incautious precipitancy of the presiding authorities.

In conformity with their undisguised and indiscreet predilection for the issue of Peers and Parliamentarians, they invested the ill-fated B—e with the onerous honours of command, merely as a pretext for providing him with an irresistible claim upon their impartial distribution of preferment. The injudicious ardour of his friends went still farther: in order to enhance his plea for speedy promotion, the vessel selected for this favoured claimant was fitted up as a fire-ship, for the purpose of destroying an enemy's frigate upon the opposite coast. In this fitting up, I understand, the stability of the brig was entirely overlooked, and she was rendered so top-heavy, that it required all the watchful caution and ability of a first-rate seaman to keep her upon her legs. Such, then, was the termination of poor B—e's young career, offering a painful but salutary lesson, backed by a crying, fearful warning, to those who suffer the idle clamour for patronage and favour to interfere with positive duties, and bias them in the disposal of important trusts. Such proceedings are not only pregnant with direful mischief to the flattered individual, but the ramifications of the glaring evil extend themselves far, wide, and deep into the mass of humanity.

B—e perished not alone; in his ruin was involved loss of life to one hundred and twenty officers and seamen, upon whom, again, rested the fate, happiness, and fortunes of so great a number of helpless creatures, that we cannot but shudder at the awful responsibility that man entails upon himself, who, in the plenitude of a discretionary but vitally momentous power, suffers his better sense to be warped, and his actions stultified, by a base truckling to the pernicious domination of place and party.

Let not the distinguished person who guides the helm of the naval interests and national pride of this country, prostitute himself to the pitiful intrigues of ministerial cabals or political prejudices! Let him stand boldly aloof from all such chicanery, and do justice to himself and to his country, by fearlessly discharging the duties of his high office. Let him distrust the claims of applicants, if supported from a suspicious quarter; and, in every case, let him pause and investigate, ere with a stroke of his pen he signs the parchment which is intended to lead to the honour and promotion of one person, but which may prove the warrant for the premature dissolution of hundreds of his fellow creatures!

It required no extraordinary depth of observation, nor the gift of prophecy, to foretell the unhappy fate of our luckless lieutenant, should he ever be destined to command. Peculiar circumstances connected him intimately with myself, and had he listened to the dictates of friendship, and abandoned those of patronage, he would have quitted a service for which he was in every way unsuited, and in all probability would have been spared an early tomb.

Experience has convinced me that many of our ships are lost from the want of proper and timely precaution and presence of mind. The latter quality is a precious gift, invaluable to the person so favoured, and not less so to those who are taught to depend upon their captain for guidance in the hour of danger: let the commanding officer then betray but one alarmed glance, or discover vacillation of purpose, and hesitation in the execution of that purpose, the crew in nine cases out of ten may be considered doomed men; fear and want of confidence become epidemic, and riot with noxious influence in the iron frames of these hitherto sturdy beings, who lose under the withering grasp all mental energy and power of action. Such is the despotic force of habit, that, should any officer among them rise superior to this prostration of mind and discern the proper and only course to be pursued, ere he can summon resolution to break through the trammels necessarily prescribed by naval discipline, and virtually suspend the authority of the captain, the favourable moment for the trial of skill may have passed away: hope buries itself in despair; and they fall a sacrifice, not to the glory of their country, but to the irresolution of one man, placed over them by the partial agents of a confiding nation!

There are indeed too often cases which no human foresight can avert, or prudence baffle; where the skill of man is but as a passing meteor to sparkle on ocean's tempestuous tide; yet leaves its powerful and lasting effects upon the well-governed mind, which, rising superior to the deprecating influence of particular events, rests secure in the belief that the whole is ordained for the best. The vast machine of the universe stops not to save a fly from being crushed beneath its wheels; and though men and animals innumerable are destroyed every day, yet the grand rotatory motion, and the unconquerable laws of nature, swerve not from their appointed course, but, heedless of the destruction they may carry in their train, continue to fulfil the all-wise intentions of their omnipotent Author.

The wounded feelings of irritated nature are soothed as we turn with glowing pride to the page of history which records the noble display and presence of mind evinced by Captain Hickey, on the occasion of the loss of his Majesty's ship Atalanta. Can there be a more strikingly illustrative example of the happy effects arising from the combined influence of decision, nerve, and confidence? He has afforded us a beacon of light and strength as to what may be successfully performed even when suddenly plunged into an apparently hopeless situation: it would be criminal did we not carefully treasure in our memories this brilliant achievement of our brother officer, and it will be doubly so, if we neglect to profit by it whenever unhappily we may be environed by similar perils. With a less decided character, what would have been the fate of that persevering, obedient, dauntless crew? They were surrounded by death's appalling terrors, but they knew and relied upon the superior powers of their commanding officer, and those natural terrors were absorbed in the prompt alacrity with which they executed the calm and confident orders issued by him from time to time as his reason suggested and the difficulties of their position required.

The hope of life, the certainty of death, were so fearfully balanced, that it wanted but the demur of a moment to turn the scale in favour of the latter; the good genius of hope prevailed. The possession of life is a boon so prized by poor mortals, that few are inclined to abandon themselves to despair whilst a shadow of chance exists of combating the force of circumstances. I envy the retrospective feelings of Captain Hickey upon this glorious triumph of human skill and decision of purpose over the adverse chances of a wayward destiny; they must be as a lantern to his path through life, and if the prayers and blessings of the families of the men preserved by his means have not been murmured in his ear, yet have they ascended to a higher source, whence retributive justice follows, sooner or later, the good or evil actions of mankind.*

Perhaps there is no situation in life which peremptorily demands so large a share of self-possession as the career of sailors. It is a quality that belongs exclusively neither to sex nor station; it depends much upon the natural temperament of the body, and much upon the moral cultivation of the mind. It arises from a steady equanimity, which enables a man in every situation, (whether the danger be imminent or remote, or whatever may be the circumstances that call for its presence,) to exert his reasoning powers with coolness and instant decision, according to the exigencies of the case in which he may be required to act a part.

It is to be supposed that sailors are bold and hardy by nature; the duties of their profession,

* See Captain Hall's account of this shipwreck, vol. i. p. 266. —Fragments of Voyages and Travels.

and the constant perils by which they are surrounded, lead to such an inference. It is, then, reasonable to expect, that men so initiated should in extreme cases be calm, prompt, and decisive; that they should be prepared to encounter the dangers of wreck, fire, and other disasters with firmness, and to oppose to their often fatal consequences ready ingenuity of design and steadiness of purpose. If these are the attributes which we would fain believe stamp the character of British sailors in general, we are at a loss to imagine how men who are aware of their deficiency on these points, can conscientiously undertake the government and charge of a ship, when they know not how soon they may be summoned to the performance of duties beyond their ability and moral power of control.

CHAPTER II.

Activity of our First Lieutenant—Arrive off the Island of St. Jago—A strange Schooner—Precautions against a suspected danger—Amusement at St. Jago—Hospitality of a Portuguese Peasant—Fishing at Porto Praya—Embarkation of Cannon—Anchor in Fayal Bay—A Dangerous Situation—Return to Portsmouth—Appointed to take charge of the East India Convoy—Interference of the Leadenhall-street Establishment—Difficulties attending the charge of a Convoy—Join Sir S. Hood's Squadron—Peak of Teneriffe—Loss of three men by falling overboard—Reflections—Repair to Madeira—A bill for Breakfast—Diving—A narrow Escape.

The activity of our first lieutenant, who was as thorough and good a seaman as could be picked out in his Majesty's navy, was conspicuously shown upon the occasion mentioned in the last chapter; he took charge of refitting and repairing the injured transport, which we kept in tow:—the weather was fine, and in one day a new mizen-mast was shipped, made out of one of our hand masts, and every thing on board of her all a-tanto, and better fitted than before the accident occurred.

After much beating about, we at length got into the trade winds, and in due time arrived within sight of the Island of St. Jago, the principal of the Cape de Verds.

The preparation for entering Porto Praya Bay, and bringing the convoy to an anchor there, had so absorbed the attention of the signal officers on board the Commodore, that a strange schooner which had joined the fleet during the night was unobserved by him. The other men-of-war thought it a work of supererogation to draw the attention of the commanding officer to a stranger that was within a mile or two of him; fancying it possible and probable she had been visited during the night. The subtle stranger kept on the same course as ourselves in the midst of the convoy, and stood into the bay. We had just anchored on the eastern side when the gentleman passed ahead of us within half pistol-shot; and to the astonishment of the whole fleet, having entered upon neutral ground, he hoisted French colours, and took up his anchorage within the whole of the convoy. She was a slaver, and the master, finding himself just before daybreak unexpectedly in the midst of an English fleet, wisely adopted the bold and masterly expedient of steering the same course, and, observing that they were bound into the bay, accompanied them: this being a neutral port, placed him in safety. The Jackdaw schooner, which had separated during the night, corresponding to the stranger in colour and appearance, the signal officer was deceived, and led to believe the number of the fleet correct. It was so perfectly ludicrous to see this little craft setting at defiance an array of line-of-battle ships, that any annoyance we might experience was disregarded in the admiration we felt for the tact and presence of mind exhibited by the Frenchman. As the safety of the fleet might have been compromised by permitting the exit of this intruder, the Commodore contented himself with taking the precaution of unhanging his rudder and taking it on board one of the ships: this was certainly an equivocal act in a neutral port, but *necessitas non habet legem.*

Some good grounds for suspicion, I believe, of a French squadron of far superior strength being in pursuit of the expedition, caused the adoption of measures not altogether compatible with the line of strict neutrality. The heavy ordnance were landed, and batteries erected around the bay in the strongest positions, and the men-of-war so disposed as to present the most formidable front to an attacking enemy.

In the mean time the work of watering and refitting went on. Many of the troops were landed, with most of their wives, for the purpose of presiding over the washing-tubs; a regular bivouac was formed among the few cocoa-nuts and plantain trees that grew in the vicinity of the beach. This island has been so often described, with a happy exposé of its ridiculous military establishment, that I shall leave the hackneyed subject altogether.

During our tiresome stay at St. Jago, I joined some of my messmates in the amusement of shooting Guinea fowl, or, more properly speaking, in an attempt to shoot them. Armed with ship's muskets, three of us wiseacres started off on as broiling a day as the tropics can boast, for the place described as the resort of these birds. The country consists of a succession of hills, the scanty herbage of which was completely scorched; not a blade of green grass was to be seen, nor the friendly shelter of a solitary tree. Vainly did we search for some less exposed spot, as the means of affording us some minutes' repose from the penetrating rays of the fiery luminary, which received additional and overwhelming power from the aridity of the soil.

We set out for a day's sport; it was likely to end in any thing but sport to us;—but what will not a set of harem-scarem Middies attempt, after being cooped up for months in a cockpit? Our ardour for the chase had insensibly cooled, and continued to abate as the sun drew forth in streams the exhaling moisture from every pore of our bodies. We should have wisely abandoned farther pursuit of our game, had not a flock of Guinea fowl unfortunately started up, and dipping the valley alighted on the adjoining hill. The sight of the birds renewed our expiring ardour; and down we descended into the valley, and toiled up the rugged ascent of the opposite hill, sufficiently alive to the animating feeling of competition as to who should get the first shot at the game, which we now considered as safe as if it had been in our bags. Spreading ourselves in line, we cautiously and softly approached the spot where the birds had been marked down, determined upon destruction.

"You fire at those to the right, M—; I'll take the centre; and you, S—, knock down as many as you can to the left:" such were the directions whispered in a low tone by the leader and planner of the expedition. But though we were fully sensible that the rogues made good use of their wings in flying from their enemies, we had not taken into consideration that they were equal adepts in the use of their legs, which we now discovered had carried them off to a considerable distance. Our disappointment was soon mitigated by getting a sight of them on the bare soil.

"There they are—there they are," and again we gave chase; but before we had traversed half the distance, they took wing and glided over to the opposite eminence. "Mark! mark! I have them exactly," and again we trudged up hill and down hill with the same tantalizing result, until they had led us a dance that completely exhausted us;

and I verily believe that we should have paid dearly for our frolic, had not our good genius discovered to us in the last valley a hut belonging to one of the natives. Consumed by a devouring, agonizing thirst, we with difficulty dragged our weary limbs to the door, and fell prostrate on the floor; the only cry our parched tongues could utter was "Aqua, aqua." Our kind-hearted host, however, gave us each a delicious draught of goat's milk, and administered all in his power to our relief.

Our perspiration had been literally dried up by the burning fever brought on by over exertion, but it now became more profuse, and delivered us from the pernicious effects of our rash folly. We could only communicate with our host by signs, and, having tolerably recovered ourselves, we made him comprehend the place where His Majesty's muskets had been unceremoniously dropped, and despatched him for them. In the course of an hour the honest Portuguese had restored them to us; but to shoulder these heavy concerns, with the long walk before us, was out of the question. A rest of six hours, with a hospitable and grateful supply of fruit from this really worthy being, enabled us to proceed on our journey homewards when the sun had quitted the valley; and with the assistance of our host's quadrupeds, by the silvery light of a beautiful moon, we succeeded in reaching our ships in safety, heartily rejoiced that our foolish excursion had ended so harmlessly. A shore-boat conveyed us on board, where we were greeted with a sharp shower of squibs and jokes by our disappointed messmates.

The night was calm, and not a ripple disturbed the surface of the sea. The peculiar transparency of the waters in these regions was on this evening so strikingly beautiful, that our in-shore anchor, which was lying in seventeen fathoms water, was as distinctly conspicuous as if it had been hanging at the bows.

A great quantity of fish may be obtained here, but during the day, or moonlight nights, there is no chance of success with the seine. We repeatedly tried our luck at an excellent small sandy bay, admirably adapted for that purpose, a little to the eastward of Porto Praya; but with little effect until we hit upon the plan of lighting a large fire, on dark nights, in the centre of the bay, close to the water's edge, when by shooting the net in a semicircle outside the fire, the quantity of fish caught was immense.

The fleet remained here nearly a month, when the different batteries erected on our arrival were dismantled, and the pieces embarked on board the ordnance transports. On bringing off some of the cannon the evening before our departure, by some unfortunate negligence on the part of the lieutenant, Lord N—, two of the twenty-four pounders were deposited in thirteen fathoms water. The charge of recovering them was made over to our first-lieutenant, who succeeded in raising them from their oozy bed in the course of two or three hours, much to the relief of the Commander-in-chief of the land forces, and to those concerned in the detention of the squadron and fleet for another twenty-four hours.

On getting outside the bay of Porto Praya, we parted company from the Commodore, taking the Ganges under our orders. After running to the westward of the whole group, we hauled up to the northward. In the course of a fortnight we came in sight of the lofty Peak of Pico, towering above the clouds: my thoughts naturally reverted to the time when I first left England, to the changes that had taken place in my own mind and prospects, and to the many public events that had transpired since the Phaeton lay becalmed under its magnificent peak.

We anchored in Fayal bay for the purpose of procuring refreshments. At sun-set the wind set right into the bay, and kept increasing; at midnight it blew a hard gale: it had attained such a height that it became dangerous for the ship to remain any longer in the same position. Preparations were immediately made for getting out to sea; the close-reefed top-sails were set, and the yards braced up to cast to starboard. When all was ready and the order given to cut the cable, the wind was about a point on the larboard bow; the last strand of the cable had scarcely been cut, when the wind suddenly chopped round six points on the starboard bow. We were now in a most perilous state; before the yards could be braced round, we made such a stern board that we could not weather the northern bluff of the bay: the only practicable alternative was instantly adopted, by letting go the other bower anchor, and taking in the sails as quickly as possible; fortunately, she brought up with her stern close to the breakers. In this anxious situation we remained till morning, when the dangers that surrounded us were disagreeably visible, and they were quite enough to have daunted one of less nerve than Captain C—. The immediate neighbourhood of the peak of Pico accounts for the sudden changes of wind that take place when blowing from the direction of the mountain, as was then the case; shifting from one side to the other in the course of a few seconds.

The Ganges, which by good fortune had not reached the anchorage the preceding evening, but now appeared in the offing, was directed by signal to take up an anchorage in a line with ourselves outside the headlands, ready to assist us whenever a favourable opportunity should ensure the bettering of ourselves. During the forenoon the Sibylle frigate appeared outside the bay, and, while we were lying at anchor in a gale of wind, was becalmed not three miles off, the breezes from the peak passing over her, and descending upon us in all their force. At noon the weather moderated sufficiently to allow the Ganges to assist us. By veering away three or four cables, and then sending us the end of her stream cable, we succeeded in lifting our own anchor, and in getting clear of a danger that at one time assumed an alarming and hopeless aspect; but *Nil desperandum* is the sailor's motto.

We returned to Portsmouth, and were shortly appointed to take charge of the East India convoy, as well as any other vessels willing to have the advantage of our protection.

The sovereign Directors of the Leadenhall-street establishment had been accustomed to send to the captains of His Majesty's ships appointed to take charge of their vessels, a certain code of instructions and signals to be used in lieu of those supplied by Government. Fully possessed with a keen sense of their own importance, they unwittingly forwarded a letter inclosing the said signals to Captain C—, with *directions* for their application. They could not have hit upon a man less likely to comply with directions coming from such a quarter; by return of post their signals, instructions, and directions were returned, with a letter setting forth the absurdity of their pretensions in issuing such a document, and containing a cutting reprimand upon their assumption of dictation. The select few doubtless opened their eyes wide at this impugnment of their supremacy, but they wisely took the hint, and from that period may be dated the abolition of their edicts for the guidance of His Majesty's officers.

On arriving in sight of Madeira, we made over the command to the senior Company's officer, and left them to pursue their route, while we bent our course to Funchal Roads. There we met Sir Samuel Hood, under whose orders we were to cruise, in company with three other line-of-battle ships, for some months off the Canary Islands.

Of all the duties that devolve upon the captains of His Majesty's ships, the charge of a convoy is perhaps the most onerous and annoying. The difficulty of making the masters attend to their instructions, and the necessary observance of the signals made to them, can scarcely be conceived. No sooner is one stray sheep brought into the flock, than another starts off; one vessel makes too much sail, another too little; while you are employed in towing up a dull sailer into the body of the convoy, others will run so far ahead as to oblige you to chase and bring them back again. The East India ships being commanded by a superior class of men, approaching the discipline and order of men of war, are particularly attentive, and never give any trouble; but with other merchant-vessels it is one constant scene of toil, trouble, and vexation, unless well regulated at the commencement, and the orders of the Commodore are carried into effect. The responsibility is great, and if any of the unruly fold are missing through the obstinacy or ill conduct of the masters, the owners and underwriters are too apt to lay the blame upon the officer in charge of them. Too much credit cannot be given to men by whose judicious arrangements and watchful attention a convoy is conducted in safety to its destination. The plan generally adopted by Captain C— was to make the dullest-sailing ship the leading one of the convoy, making her carry all possible sail with safety, and never permitting any of the others to pass her beam; whenever this occurred, a shot was fired across the offending party's hawse, the expense of which was paid for by the master. As a captain of a man-of-war can only be actuated by a sincere and anxious desire for the safety and protection of the commercial interests of his country, the underwriters at Lloyd's cannot pay too much attention to any representation he may think it necessary to make to that body respecting the conduct of individuals entrusted with the charge of their merchantships.

The squadron having assembled, we proceeded to the southward. When within a hundred and ten miles of the Peak of Teneriffe, the weather remarkably clear, and the time near sunset, it appeared to lift its lofty summit far above the horizon, resembling a thin blue cloud, the faint outlines of which were scarcely two shades darker than the heavens. It recalled forcibly to my mind the departed hero Nelson : he had towered high above his fellows, as the lofty pinnacle before us rose superior in height to the islands around it: it was at its base he lost his right arm; piecemeal did he offer himself to the service and glory of his country, and consummated the sacrifice in a halo of brightness which will shed its piercing rays into the darkest recesses of futurity.

>   ———" To live with fame
> The Gods allow to many; but to die
> With equal lustre, is a blessing Heaven
> Selects from all the choicest boons of fate,
> And with a sparing hand on few bestows."

A fatality appeared to attend us during this unfortunate cruise; eight or ten men were lost overboard. Of all the melancholy scenes which beset the sailor's life, I know of none so deeply distressing as that which attends the loss of life to men by falling overboard. In the course of one stormy night, whilst close reefing the topsails, three unfortunate beings, by a sudden change of wind, were for ever severed from their companions. I cannot better describe this painful occurrence, than by availing myself of the beautiful lines of Falconer, who was himself fated to perish amidst the horrors of that element which he has so pathetically and ably described:—

> " While from its margin, terrible to tell,
>   Three sailors with their gallant boatswain fell;
>   Torn with resistless fury from their hold,
>   In vain their struggling arms the yard enfold;
>   In vain to grapple flying cords they try;
>   The cords, alas! a solid gripe deny!

Thrown on the midnight surge, with panting breath
They cry for aid, and long contend with death.
High o'er their heads the rolling billows sweep,
And down they sink in everlasting sleep.
Bereft of power to help, their comrades see
The wretched victims die beneath the lee;
With fruitless sorrow their lost state bemoan,
Perhaps a fatal prelude to their own!"

It was dark, and we were unable to afford any assistance to the drowning men. I will not now expatiate upon the mischief that often proceeds from the well-meant but injudicious struggling and rivalry that instantly prevails when a man is overboard, as to who shall be first in the work of humanity, but which end is at times sadly defeated by the total absence of method and purpose. The original evil is not unfrequently aggravated by an increase of victims, the result of confusion and mismanagement. I once suffered so excruciatingly in mind after a deplorable accident of this nature (but which, not coming within the scope of this work, will not now be commented on,) that, should I ever again command one of His Majesty's ships, I shall give my best attention to this important subject, and endeavour to devise some means, not only to lessen the risk attendant on these frequent mischances, but to encourage as much as possible the art of swimming, which is an absolutely necessary part of a sailor's education. The sea is our element, and we should swim upon its surface, and dive into its bosom, with as much *sang-froid* as we pace the deck, or lightly trip on shore.

At the conclusion of the cruise, which was barren in interest, we again repaired to Madeira. Here the parties of shore-going reckless reefers enacted their usual part in a gallop up to the Convent and down again, at the risk of breaking their necks, accompanied by their convoy, the master of the poor animal holding on by the tail. A good breakfast being leisurely despatched, we called for our bill, and were not slightly startled to find it amounted to fourteen thousand five hundred and odd reas!

"Fourteen thousand devils!" exclaimed all aghast: "what does the fellow mean?"

The waiter could not speak English or French, nor any of us Portuguese; our host was accordingly ordered up. Meanwhile we were comparing notes, and adding up the sum total of cash possessed by us *en masse*. The lowest dixieme in the numerical table, which the dollars corresponded to, was alarming. We were agreeably surprised by the landlord proclaiming that the thousands which had so scared us, reduced into dollars, would amount to eighteen : a sum far exceeding the demands of equity, but which at that moment appeared trifling, compared to our previously excited fears :—we paid it without a demur.

During our stay here I very narrowly escaped becoming food for fishes. The first lieutenant had given us the jolly-boat to proceed on a bathing expedition, and we pulled to a rock not far from the Loo. Two of the crew were in the boat, one of whom was an East Indian: he remarked to us, that when in the act of diving, if the hands were joined and raised above the head, we should shoot up to the surface without moving a limb. The whole party had begun dressing themselves when I determined upon having another dive, to try the East Indian's plan. I leaped off the rock into twenty fathoms, and, ambitious to outdo all my messmates in the length of time I could remain under water, I allowed myself to sink to a certain depth, from which I fancied I could hold out till I again reached the surface; accordingly I adopted the Indian's plan of holding my arms over my head, and supposed I was fast ascending, when, in point of fact, I was rapidly descending. Greatly exhausted, I began to strike out; but, before I attained the surface, I had taken in such a quantity of water, that I was nearly senseless, and had no power to keep myself afloat, and down I went again: I rose a second time, fortunately close to the rock, but in a perfectly senseless state. My companions imagined that on my first appearance I was playing a part to frighten them; but during the short interval of my second submersion they became alarmed, and, when I again rose, seized me by the arm, and hauled me into the boat. After disgorging a great quantity of the saline fluid, my senses returned. I did not recover the effects of this invasion of the deep for a month, and the pain I suffered in my ears during the passage to England, amounted at times to agony. I experienced all the sensations of death by drowning, which, by the by, I should say were not very terrible, and were it not smacking too much of Hibernia, I think I might say I have been drowned.

CHAPTER III.

Placed on board the Achille—Blockade—Master's Mates—A Cock-pit Orpheus—Fracas with the Caterer of the Mess—His complaint to the Captain—Jocular revenge of the Middies—Consequent partition of the larboard berth—Follow-my-Leader—Grampus blowing.

Captain C—, on his arrival at Plymouth, gave up the ship; and two other Middies and myself were placed on board the Achille, Sir Richard K—g, who shortly afterwards proceeded in command of a squadron off Ferrol, where the Spaniards were fitting out a squadron. Nine months did we blockade them, with nothing to relieve the monotony of the scene but the everlasting sight of Cape Prior, varied only, as the winter gales drove us to the northward or southward, by views of Cape Turiana and Cape Ortegal. Fortunately the high spirits of young blood broke through the *ennui* that must otherwise have bound us in its withering folds: what with cockpit pranks, bull dancing, the occasional fill-up of a gale of wind, and an excellent skipper, we passed away a merry winter; for to be otherwise than merry in the cockpit of the Achille, a fellow must have been made of impenetrable stuff.

The two master's mates were rather advanced in years for that rank in his Majesty's service. The senior of them had charge of the larboard berth: he had, I believe, risen from an inferior station; it was at least presumed so from the unsparing manner in which he clipped and transmogrified the King's English. His success in emerging from his primary orbit had certainly greatly tended to raise his own ideas of self-importance, and this in a much higher ratio than the turbulent reefers, over whom he presided, appeared to think admissible. His ludicrous endeavours to maintain his position, and the mischievous tricks of the boys to shake the rooted opinion he entertained of his own worth, were the cause of constant contention and excitement to the inhabitant of the lower regions.

As specimens of this class are now nearly if not quite extinct in the navy, and the redoubtable hero of the scene I am going to describe has long since disappeared from the world's stage, I shall introduce him to my readers. He was an awkward-made man, about forty years of age, but only acknowledged to be something under thirty; with a large sharp countenance deeply marked with the small-pox; altogether anything but prepossessing in his outward appearance. The only staunch ally he could boast of was his brother officer, whose *penchant* for the fine arts, in the shape of rasping catgut upon a cracked violin, though all very musical to the obtuse senses of his sympathizing friends, was any thing but harmony to the sensibly acute organs of the tormented reefers. The cockpit Orpheus was an active, well-built fellow, perfectly competent to contend with half a dozen of his younger brethren; his weighty hand, however delicately it might at times draw forth inspiring sounds, was equally capable, as many could testify, of eliciting from the unfortunate youngster who fell under his displeasure, notes as unmusical and discordant as any blatant quadruped could well produce. But for this knowledge, I suspect his solos would have been more frequently interrupted, if indeed the means of practising them had not altogether disappeared by the offending instrument and all its appurtenances being consigned to the care of the Naiads. The self-consequence of the one and the musical pretensions of the other had separated the two mates from the support or suffrages of the reefers, and accordingly an alliance, offensive and defensive, was entered into by these worthies. In consequence of this inimical state of things, they were regarded as fair play by the younger fraternity, whenever the opportunity occurred of attacking them with advantage.

Old Woollard prided himself amazingly upon his abilities as caterer, and viewed with indignant horror the attempt of any individual to interfere with his arrangements, or the presumption of questioning any item in the accounts he laid upon the table for their inspection. One of the most wicked of the cockpit wags determined not only to dispute the authority of the caterer, but to overhaul the accounts.

The shrill pipe of the boatswain had summoned

all hands to the work of mastication. Pea-soup graced the head of the table, and a dish of salt-junk, encrusted with a dark coat of saline particles, the bottom. Taking advantage of the absence of the musician, who was detained serving out the grog, the mischief-loving Mid began the attack.

" Where are the potatoes, boy ?"

" There are not no more," answered the caterer.

" Not no more, Woollard : I am glad to hear that, for two negatives make an affirmative ; then why are they not on the table ?"

" I tells you as how there are not no more ; I'll call you a thundering knowing fellow if you can make 'taties out of your negatives and your 'firmatives, as you call them."

" All our sea stock expended already ! it is impossible ; there must be some mismanagement."

" What is that ere you say, Master Nimblechops ? I advise you to lap your gruel, and not meddle with those there consarns you have no business with."

" I have paid my mess, and I have a right to know how it has been expended."

"Certainly he has,—he has," repeated the whole assembled company.

Down dropped the soup-ladle from the hands of the astonished caterer, eyeing all around with wonder and ill-concealed ire. "Why, what the h—ll are you all arter? Come, no more of your gammon, or I'll give some of you a bunch of fives instead of your 'taties."

The operations of the dinner-table were at a stand-still.

"Is that your mode of settling accounts? That won't do, Woollard; we must have it in black and white."

"I tell you what it is, young gentlemen: if you gives me any more of your slack jaw, I'll just go up to Sir Richard K—g, and see what he'll say to this here nitty—"

"Go! go! go!" resounded from all sides in universal chorus, joined in by the members of the opposite berth; and the enraged commander-in-chief of the cockpit, being unable to vent his wrath upon any particular individual, started off amidst a shower of Bravoes! which accelerated his pace to an unusual rapidity of movement. Foaming with rage he appeared on the quarter-deck; his anger had in some degree divested him of that awe in which he usually stood when he addressed his captain.

"What is the matter, Mr. Woollard?"

"Why, do you see, Sir Richard, those there young gentlemen, Mr. D–f–d and Mr. D–gl–s at the head of them, are bullying on me at no rate; I can't eat my dinner in peace, Sir Richard; they have all set-to upon me, cause as how there are no 'taties."

"Indeed, Mr. Woollard. But what have they been about? whom do you complain of in particular?"

"There are no partiklers among them; they are all alike, Sir Richard. You see it's more than three months since we left port, and it's quite an unpossible thing for the wegetables to last for ever."

It was evident that the risible faculties of Sir Richard were in danger of being excited to a pitch that might have exploded in laughter, had he not bent his steps towards his cabin while addressing the offended dignitary.

"Very true, Mr. Woollard, very true; but I have no doubt they will see the folly of such expectations: the better plan would be not to take any notice of them."

The sentry closed the cabin-door, and poor Woollard took nothing by his motion. The scene on the quarter-deck was known in the cockpit before the descent of the mate; a *chiavara* was prepared for him that any mob of Frenchmen might have envied for the effect it had upon the object it was given in honour of. Not a word was uttered as he retook his seat at the table: his own communication broke the silence.

"If any more of this here nonsense is going on, Sir Richard will bring you up, my fine lads, with a round turn double-bitted, do you see; so you had better be quiet."

And he took up his knife and fork to proceed with his dinner. One of his tormentors sang out "W," a second "double O," a third "double L,"—"A," repeated a fourth, "R," added a fifth, "D," screamed a sixth. The whole of the starboard and larboard berths having caught up the patronymic of our chief, it was rung out in such a quick succession of changes in his tortured ears, as in a sort of bewilderment he turned from the first aggressor to the second, third, and so on, for explanation of this unaccountable attack, that, unable to slide in a word amidst the deafening chorus of Wool-lard—Wool-lard—Wool-lard, the persecuted man found his only refuge and means of revenge in the discharge of a shower of biscuits and missiles at the noddles of the offending parties. Throwing a scowling look of defiance around, he darted out of the cockpit to make known to the first Lieutenant " the unpossibility of remaining in such a den as that ere larboard berth."

A regular inquiry now took place, and as the whole *posse comitatus* of the cock-pit were involved in the charge, the cause was, after a patient hearing, referred to the Captain, who decided that, as the mateys could not live in peace with the reefers, it would be necessary to divide the larboard berth; and the carpenters were immediately set to work to run up a bulk-head to separate the contending parties, the musical mate and his ally taking up their abode in the smaller one, and the discomfited reefers cramming themselves into the other.

Poor Woollard only increased his ills by the change, for the attacks upon his comfort were not only more frequent, but carried on more successfully under the cover of the bulk-head.

Follow my leader, in fine weather, was a favourite amusement of the frolicksome reefers of the Achille; there was no end to their jokes and tricks. At the close of a middle watch the leader was still showing off his agility and calling upon his followers to perform their part of the game by strictly imitating all the manœuvres he should present to them. As a finale he jumped into the windsail, and descended into the cockpit. I followed: we were ready prepared with a rope-yarn to tie up the mouth of the sail, which was quickly executed. My old friend and messmate R—ds was the first who found himself caught in the trap. "Hold fast! hold fast," came too late to be of any avail as a warning to those who were rapidly descending upon him. Up the leader and myself scampered to the quarter-deck, where under the poop-awning stood all the wash-deck buckets, ready filled with water for washing decks. In the twinkling of an eye the contents were hurled with merciless aim and relentless purpose down the windsail. "Oh G–d! oh G–d! I can't breathe. Oh! you—you'll—suffo—suffocate us; we—we are dy—dying," sputtered forth the four pendant prisoners. Down flowed another bucketful, and the hubbub in the cockpit was at its height, when flop came the whole contents of the windsail, Middies, salt-water and all, upon the cockpit-deck; the happy delivery having been effected by my friend Dick's knife, with which he cut his way through his canvass prison.

Generally speaking, I know of no ship where the Middies kept a stricter watch than on board the Achille: a breach of the observance was attended with woful effects to the lad caught napping; for as sure as the eye closed, the grampus began blowing; and what was still more disagreeable, the Captain was equally certain of hearing it.

As my land readers may not be aware of the meaning of grampus blowing, I will explain the mode usually adopted on these occasions. As soon as information is obtained of the violation of this most rigid article of war relating to sleeping upon watch, the whole band of Middies belonging to the watch assemble round the sleeping innocent, each armed with a bucket full of water. All being duly prepared, one dashes the contents of his bucket full in the face of the delinquent, loudly bawling in his ear at the same moment " A man overboard !" and before the poor devil can recover the scaring effects of the first dose, he is almost suffocated by the repeated shocks that assail him from all parts, and so bewildered and mystified that he is led to believe he is the identical fellow who is overboard. Arms and legs are seen striking out in every direction, and " Sa—sa—save me !" plaintively uttered, till the streams cease flowing, and permit the affrighted culprit to recall his scattered senses.

CHAPTER IV.

Ordered into Port—Moored in Cawsand Bay—Join Captain C—
in the Pompée—My new Messmates—Proceed off Rochfort
—Frolic in l'Isle du Rhé—A Guernsey Privateer aground—
Exertions to save her—Ordered to perform the duty of a Lieutenant—Reflections on the propriety of accustoming young
men to the command of the Deck—My new honours threatened with a speedy termination—An Accident—Inquiry and
Acquittal—Fall in with a suspicious Schooner—Rejoin the
Impetueux—Unexpected present of Wine—A strange Sail—
The Chase—The Capture—A Recognition—Sent with Lieutenant M— to take charge of the Prize—The Yellow Fever
on board her—Terrible ravage of the disease—I am seized
by the contagion—Death of Mr. Booth—The Black Vomit
My convalescence—Yellow Jack—A Presentiment—Reflections.

Orders at length arrived to send us into port, and greatly delighted we were at this change of destiny. Nine months, during which time we had never let go an anchor, was no uncommon period to remain cruising off the enemy's coast during the war. We were soon snugly moored in Cawsand Bay, fully prepared to taste the joys of the shore. Letters awaited the arrival of R—ds and myself, informing us that Captain C— was appointed to the Aboukir, seventy-four, at Chatham, and the day following we were desired by Sir Richard K—g to prepare for joining our former Captain. We joyfully set out for our new ship. Before we arrived at Chatham, Captain C— was removed to the Pompée, eighty-gun ship, at the same port, one of the finest line-of-battle ships at that time in his Majesty's service, and the very same vessel upon whose deck, some ten or eleven years prior to my present dignified introduction, I had made my *entrée* into the service tucked up under the sidesman's arm, armed with a dirk and fully accoutred in knee-breeches, cocked-hat, &c. all according to the then strict etiquette. I must have been a perfect figure of fun, and I cannot wonder that the little officer was courteously dismissed to sup porridge, and con over his *hic hæc hoc*. I now trod the deck "chewing the cud of sweet and bitter fancy;" the flavour of the first, however, predominated in the melange, as I turned my thoughts from past scenes to present prospects. My *amour propre* had been deeply gratified by receiving a higher rating, and my instalment as mate of the first watch.

Some of my new messmates were dashing blades; so, after a slight consultation, it was decided that our berth should be fitted up in a style of elegance and splendour suited to the extravagant ideas of some of its inhabitants. A most imposing display of plate was the consequence of this sage resolution; a steward was shipped, and by the favour of our Captain the berth was enlarged, and a store-room appropriated to our use.

Whether an ardent desire to show how things could be done in the cockpit, or whether the love of hospitality was the dominant reason, I cannot now take upon me to determine; but certain it is that the midshipmen of his Majesty's ship Pompée sent their compliments to the lieutenants and reefers of his Majesty's fleet then lying in Torbay, requesting the honour of their company at dinner on a specified day, (wind and weather permitting); and it is no less certain that about fifty guests were on that day assembled in the gun-room of the Pompée, which had been kindly yielded up to their use, and that mirth, good humour, and cordiality reigned paramount at the festive board. Doubtless the refined ideas and luxurious habits of the elegant young gentlemen of the flag and guard-ships of the present day would lead them to scout with indignation the claims of the Pompée's officers to distinction upon a point so peculiarly their own; nevertheless the entertainment was *recherché;* it became a nine days' wonder; and if we had any vanity, it was gratified by the encomiums we received, and the matter it furnished for conversation and discussion among our less dashing brethren in arms.

Detached from the Ushant team, we proceeded off Rochfort to watch the enemy's vessels in Aix Roads. The numerous opportunities that daily occurred of chasing the chasse-marées with the boats, made the time pass cheerily enough; they were frequently despatched at night to endeavour to cut off these coasting craft, and afforded interesting employment to the younger hands.

One dark still night I was ordered off with the barge and pinnace under my command. Placing the latter in her appointed station, I proceeded to take up mine inside l'Isle du Rhé. We were pulling with muffled oars quietly along the shore, when an old hard-a-weather boatswain's mate, who was acting coxswain for the night, requested very earnestly that I would allow him to go on shore, "just for the fun of the thing," merely to pluck a turf to show Johnny Crapaud, when day broke, that with all his patrolling he could not prevent us from landing.

" God bless you, Mr. S—, do ye now, if it is only a blade of grass."

The proposal of the veteran happening to chime in with my own foolish inclinations, the request was complied with, and the boat's head was directed to the beach, and in a few minutes her keel grated on the strand. Armed with cutlasses and pistols, we landed, leaving six hands to keep the boat afloat, and proceeded silently in a close body directly inland : the path we pursued led us to a vineyard, bounded on one side by a steep bank. I began to reflect upon the folly and danger of this inroad upon a hostile shore, without any ostensible object but the gratification of a foolish freak; when, just as I had determined to act upon the sensible resolution of beating a speedy retreat, one of my fellows having climbed the bank, sang out,

" D—n my eyes, if here arn't a parcel of woolly birds."

Up to this moment I had kept them in compact order and strict silence, but no sooner was this incautious exclamation uttered, than all broke loose from their restraint, mounted the bank, and ran off helter-skelter in chase of the supposed woolly birds. I now felt the rashness of my conduct in its fullest extent; and what would have been the result of it I cannot pretend to divine, had not the woolly birds, on close examination, turned out to be a knot of low separated bushes, which, in the haze and darkness of the night, were taken for sheep. I immediately collected my stray flock: we marched off for the boat with as much haste as our legs could carry us, and were lucky enough to reach and enter it at the precise moment the French patroles met at the point of our embarkation.

We got clear off, uninjured by the musket-shots that were sent after us, though several of them struck the boat. Most sincerely did I bless my lucky stars for having extricated me out of so foolish a scrape. The turf, and some branches of the vine, were maliciously displayed at daybreak on the boat-hook in the bow, which drew upon us the harmless fire of the fort on l'Isle du Rhé. So much for juvenile tricks.

While cruising off Rochfort, a Guernsey privateer, standing too close in shore, grounded on the Isle du Rhé; the barge was immediately despatched by Captain C— to her assistance. By the time we reached her, the ebb-tide had made, and all our exertions to get her off proved fruitless. As the water receded, our considerate lookout friends on shore brought down a couple of field pieces, by way of keeping us warm and affording us amusement. The cutter had heeled over so much to seaward, in consequence of the shores with which we had endeavoured to keep her upright giving way, that her guns were useless. Indeed, the position the Frenchmen had taken up would have effectually prevented us from annoying them had we been upon an even keel: it was a long, flat, shelving shore, so that at high water their shot barely reached us; but as the tide fell, and they became more pointed in their attentions, we found our situation by no means agreeable. To abandon the vessel without straining every nerve to save her was not a likely act of Lieutenant B—dges, who had arrived with an additional reinforcement: it was not to be thought of. Night was approaching, and ther was good reason to hope she might be so lightened before the next high water that the chances would be greatly in favour of her escape. Another boat being sent to our assistance, her guns, and the greater part of her stores, were got out. At low water she was high and dry, nearly a quarter of a mile above low water mark. It was fortunately dark; but the enemy had now advanced so near us, that every shot they fired entered the unfortunate craft. We were pretty well secured by remaining under the lee of the cutter; but, fearful of being surrounded, which manœuvre might have easily been attempted, we were obliged to throw out parties to the right and left, so that, in case of an attack of that description by superior numbers, we should have been enabled to make good our retreat to the boats. Finding no return to their fire, and every thing quiet, the Frenchmen approached with an apparent determination to get possession of the vessel. Discharging their pieces, they came on in double-quick time; but a salute of small arms drove them instantly back again, and no further attempt was made to dislodge us. We were, however, so riddled by their round shot before the flood forced them to retreat, that the privateer was done over; her bottom was regularly drilled; and the water made its way so much more rapidly into her hold than we could get clear of it, that we found ourselves under the disagreeable necessity of putting the finishing stroke to the Frenchman's work, by effectually placing her *hors du combat.* At low water the enemy took possession of her remains.

It must have been a galling spectacle to the officers of the Gallic squadron to see us taking shelter in Basque Roads from the gales outside, of which convenience we invariably availed ourselves, even striking lower yards and topmasts whenever the gale rendered such a precaution necessary. The Impetueux became our Commodore, and in company with her and the Theseus we continued to cruise off this coast.

During the latter part of our cruise, I was ordered to perform the duty of a Lieutenant. The charge of an eighty-gun ship raised me a hundred per cent. in my own estimation : to stand high in the opinion of my Captain was one of the leading marks of my ambition, and this confidence on his part appeared to me a sign of especial grace and favour.

I am of opinion that there cannot be a more judicious plan adopted than that of accustoming young men (worthy of confidence) to the command of the deck: it provokes a laudable degree of ambition and emulation in the person selected; it early habituates him to the observance of self-command and to the exercise of authority over others; and it tends to allay those feverish feelings of irritation that are too often engendered by the dilatory acknowledgment of services that a long series of years of patient merit justly entitle to reward.

The above remark refers more particularly to passed midshipmen; but youngsters who possess abilities, steadiness, and an ardent desire to excel in their profession, cannot too soon, under proper surveillance, be included in this desirable arrangement. By far the greater number of lieutenants never tread the deck as officers of the watch until they do so by virtue of their commission. One would imagine that the precious piece of parchment had talismanic properties; that it could convert the dunderhead into the officer, and endow him at once with the requisite quantum of abilities and experience.

My new honours were threatened with a very speedy termination. It was the middle watch, and we were sailing in line with the Impetueux and Theseus, when the Commodore made the signal to tack in succession. We followed in his wake, but the Theseus, who, previously to our going about, was to windward of her station three or four points on our weather quarter, instead of going astern of us, according to the signal, and then tacking, endeavoured to pass between us and the Commodore, though our jib-boom was nearly over the taffrail of the Impetueux. Not supposing the Theseus would persist in this mad course, and knowing I was in my proper station, I stood on. Too late she perceived her error, and altered her course to pass astern. Finding that she must inevitably come in contact with us, I put the helm down to lessen the shock, and slap she took us on the quarter; her jib-boom passing abaft the mizen-rigging, knocking away the quarter-boat, and dealing out sundry other damage and detriment to his Majesty's ship Pompée. The

Captain was on deck in a trice. Believing, at the first glance of affairs, that I was to blame, he was on the point of opening out his lower-deckers upon me, when I requested him to take notice of the Commodore's position. The storm that was ready to fall heavily upon my shoulders, was shifted to those of the unfortunate lieutenant of the offending ship. Next day an inquiry took place, when I was perfectly acquitted by the evidence of the officer of the watch on board the Impetueux. The culprit lieutenant got off with a few days' arrest, and the payment of the value of the jib-boom.

Despatched off Cordovan light-house, we fell in with a suspicious schooner, to which we gave chase. It blew so hard that we nearly buried her under the heavy press of sail she carried on. She was within gun-shot, and in a fair way of falling into our clutches, when the wind suddenly shifting brought her on the weather bow, and fell to a light air. Whilst we were lying pretty nearly motionless on the water, the schooner was creeping away to windward; at dark we lost sight of her. We afterwards learned that she was a Spaniard, richly freighted with dollars, and succeeded in getting into port.

On rejoining the Impetueux we were ordered into Plymouth, at which place we fitted out for the West Indies. The station allotted to us was not highly relished by the major part of the officers, but to the young hands it presented the features of novelty: a desideratum quite sufficient to secure their approbation; any thing was preferable to sailing in line off Ushant. We touched at Madeira, and this time I had the wisdom to arm myself with a letter of introduction to one of the principal mercantile houses in the island. From these gentlemen I received the most hospitable attention, such as induces me to recommend to all lieutenants and middies the adoption of a similar politic measure.

On the morning of our departure from Funchal Roads, I was surprised at the announcement of " A cask of wine is alongside for Mr. S—."

"For me, quartermaster? no such good luck, it is a mistake."

" Box your trotters, master Jemmy, and see what is in the wind," sang out a reefer ; and as

I got upon the quarter-deck, a note agreeably explained the mystery. It was a present of fine old bottled Madeira from my kind friends on shore. Having seen it safely landed on the main-deck, I lost no time in gladdening the hearts of my messmates with the pleasing intelligence of there being no quiz in the case, but *bona fide* the juice of the generous grape. So loudly was it praised, and so amicably was it discussed, that, alas! the remembrance of its balmy fragrance alone remained when we anchored in Carlisle Bay at Barbadoes.

We were within a few days of our destination, and were rolling down the trades, when at six in the morning a strange sail was discovered on our starboard quarter, apparently in chase of us; we immediately hauled to the wind. This manœuvre disenchanted the golden visions of the stranger, and, finding us likely to prove an awkward customer, he likewise hauled upon a bowline. The chase now began. The lower yards of the pursued (evidently a man-of-war brig) could only be seen from the main-top; but her manœuvres, and the cut of her sails, at once announced her nation. As the sun rose in the heavens, the wind increased, and we had already gained considerably on the chase, when she was under the necessity of reefing in consequence of the strong squalls and fiery trade wind. This was just the weather in which the old Pompée shone to the greatest advantage, and we hailed the increasing gusts with pleasure. All hands were kept upon deck ready to shorten sail at an instant's notice. The brig being to windward was a certain guide to us as to the strength of the squalls, and we were prepared to act accordingly. By noon we had her hull up from the deck: she carried on most nobly; her spars bent like bows before she yielded to the blast. As soon as her top-sails were observed coming down, every man was on the alert, and the instant the squall struck us the top-gallant-sails were furled, and the top-sails down in a trice. The moment its force was expended, up they flew to the mast-heads, and the upper sails were again expanded to the breeze. It was one of the most beautiful and soul-stirring chases it has ever been my fortune to witness.

The little craft was clearly overpressed; not the

vantage ground of a hair's breadth was lost on our side. In one of the heavy squalls her lee main-top-sail sheet was carried away, and the sail fluttered in ribbons. We made sure of our prey— "She is our's to a certainty,"—when that certainty vanished by the smartness of the Frenchman, who in double-quick time bent another main-top-sail. The Pompée's men had scarcely taken in another reef, when our skilful foe was observed sheeting home and hoisting away again. It required no great sagacity to discover that her commander was a practically good seaman, who knew full well how to manage his dashing little barky. In a short time, away went both his foretop-sail sheets. "She cannot escape now—it is impossible."— "By heavens! he has secured his canvass this time—there he is hauling home his sheets again." —"Well done—gallantly done, Johnny Crapaud,—the Devil favours his own offspring."— "Blow, good breezes, blow," (the wind was beginning to lull.) "Shake out a reef of the topsails."

And now the fears of losing the brig began to assume a palpable form, as she was observed to hold her own. No sooner were our men laid out upon the top-sail yards, than the brig's men appeared to be occupied with the like duty. "He is determined to give us a run for it."—"Blow breezes, blow," was again heard murmuring around, and, by way of coaxing the airs of heaven, the master and first lieutenant were whistling to the wind, in tune something similar to that adopted by ostlers to their horses. All our whistling and coaxings failed in propitiating the wind deities. The sun declined, the wind dropped, and the Frenchman remained upon the gaining side; there was no moon, and the distance was too great between us to admit of the hope of keeping him in sight when night should close in. The ship was kept rapt full to get on her beam, as affording us the best chance of seeing her with the night-glasses. Not a vestige of the chase could be discovered an hour after sunset. A further pursuit was considered both hopeless and unprofitable by the disappointed officers.

We expected the hammocks to be piped down, and the ship to be kept on her course again; but Captain C— had acquired too much experience of our cunning adversary's shiftings and doublings to resign prematurely a quarry in every way worthy our attention. The plan he pursued, displayed the sound judgment that always guided his conduct in cases of difficulty and uncertainty, at once inspiring hope, security, and confidence in those around him. He noted the spot where we had first fallen in with the brig, and her precise situation when last seen; and concluded that the wary Frenchman would stand on under all sail till nine o'clock, then tack, and bear up before the wind to take his original position. Accordingly, at the hour he expected the chase to tack, we went about, and shortened sail to the topsails. The wind had previously fallen to a light breeze. In due time we edged away to meet him, on the supposed line of his course. All hands were ready stationed to make sail in an instant; the main-deck guns were cleared away; officers and men were peering in all directions, endeavouring to penetrate the darkness that surrounded the vessel. Meanwhile the captain, who had retired for a few minutes to consult the chart, upon which he had marked the expected point of meeting, returned to the quarter-deck. " Keep a sharp look-out on the weather bow," said he,— and turning round to the officers, added, " If my conjectures are correct, we ought to be close on board of her."

" Take the night-glass forward, Mr. B—g—d, and keep sweeping the horizon about four points on the bow."

" Ay, ay, sir."—But before that officer had reached the forecastle, the welcome cry of a strange sail to windward was heard from the cat-head. In an instant the outlines of her extended canvass were visible, standing forth in strong relief from the dark background of a mass of vapoury clouds. The top-gallant sails and fore-sail were speedily set, and the Pompée in a line with the stranger: the enemy was thus brought immediately under the muzzle of our guns. At the first shot, he prudently let fly every tack and sheet, and hove-to; we were equally expeditious, and both vessels were lying so close that any attempt on the part of the brig to escape would have subjected her to certain destruction. The first boat brought on board the captain, who was minus an arm by our countrymen on a former occasion. The prize was a fine man-of-war brig, Le Pylade, carrying sixteen thirty-two pound carronades and one hundred and nine men. She had run successfully the whole of the war, had just left Martinique, and was an excellent sailer, of which qualification we had incontestable proof. She had afforded us a chase that might have inspired and interested the most fastidious amateur in these matters. Both vessels were so admirably managed, the possible loss and probable advantages so nicely balanced on both sides, that I do not think either of them could be said to win upon the other in point of skill during the whole of the morning's manœuvres. Stratagem eventually favoured us, and the neat finale to the pursuit was sagaciously planned and successfully executed. The underwriters at Lloyd's had paid dearly for the various depredations of this industrious little brig. The poor Frenchman, it appeared, did not perceive us till we were actually alongside of him, and the whistling of the shot between his masts dispelled his dreams of security. At the very moment they fell into our power, they were congratulating themselves upon their escape. On looking over a log-book belonging to one of the officers, in which his hopes and fears during the day had been carefully registered, I observed that at five o'clock, when the wind had fallen and the brig appeared to have rather gained upon us, the Frenchman had written down, " Dieu merci, nous ne serons pas pris aujour-d'hui. Adieu! Jean Boull—adieu ! ros bif !"

Our third lieutenant had, some years prior to this capture, been severely wounded in a cutting-out expedition. He had gained the enemy's decks and was engaged hand-to-hand with a French officer, when the latter drew his pistol and fired ; the ball passed through both cheeks without any material injury, but the muzzle of the weapon was so close, that the charge of powder was buried in his face, which remaining there ever after, clearly stamped a receipt in full for the value of gunpowder received. At the breakfast-table the following morning our lieutenant recognized in one of the French officers the destroyer of his beauty. Whatever enmity might have subsisted at the time of deadly strife, no traces of such feeling could be discovered in the hearty shake of the hand and warm greetings that instantly took place between the once belligerent parties.

I was sent with thirty-two hands, under Lieutenant M‑l‑d, to take charge of the prize. In the hurry and confusion of sending the prisoners on board the Pompée, the French surgeons were moved off with the rest, and it was not until we had made sail in company with our own ship, that we discovered several of the crew were ill below with the yellow fever. We had soon a melancholy proof of its formidable presence. During the latter part of the middle watch, two poor wretches ascended the deck in a state of appalling madness; they were secured after a desperate struggle, in which they showed a degree of strength and power credible only to those who are accustomed to witness the paroxysms of insanity. In yielding to the superiority of numbers, their mortal existence passed away with the annihilation of the supernatural energy that supported it. Before daybreak, we had consigned three victims to the deep.

As day dawned we made the signal to the Pompée for medical aid. The assistant who was in consequence sent on board not understanding the French language, I accompanied him round to the hammocks of the suffering Frenchmen. I was happily free from all fear of infection. We had certainly heard enough at home of the pestilential fever that sometimes swept away whole ships' companies, and had little heeded it; but now that we beheld its ravaging effects, and its dreadful concomitant, raging madness, it was sufficient to turn our congratulations into condolence, and to congeal the warm current of our blood. In forty-eight hours we were at an anchor in Carlisle bay, and I was left commanding officer of the prize for the purpose of clearing her; she having been immediately purchased into the service by the Commander-in-chief. Brief was the time that intervened before six of our own men were sent on board the Pompée, attacked with fever. The seventeen Frenchmen were all dead. The succeeding morning eight more were added to the fatal list, and conveyed direct to the shore. The prize was very shortly after our arrival ready to be given up to the lieutenant who was to commission her, at which period every soul of the prize crew, excepting myself, had been transported to the hospital; and half of them were already numbered with the dead.

As a small quantity of gunpowder yet remained on board the prize, I was to return in the morning to superintend its conveyance to St. Anne's. Of the thirty-three men who had quitted the Pompée in the enjoyment of life, hope, and health, to take possession of Le Pylade, ere the glorious sun had five times dipped the western horizon, I alone returned, a solitary dejected being, to our ship! But I was not to pass unharmed through this terrible ordeal; the infection was then insidiously lurking in my veins. That same night the most frightful dreams haunted my imagination, and the quartermaster's report, at daylight, that the boat was manned for me, came like a respite from the torments of the infernal regions. As I made my appearance on the quarter-deck, the lieutenant of the watch rallied me on my inflamed and jaded looks: suspecting I was not the thing, he inquired, "What ails you, Jemmy?"

"I am not well; my head burns like fire."

"Oh! nonsense! fancy you are going to have the fever, my boy!"

" Indeed I am afraid I have it!"

" That's right, my fine fellow! only think so, and you'll do!" and he endeavoured to laugh me out of my feelings. I felt nettled, and remarked that I had not complained in order to avoid the morning's duty allotted to me.

I pushed off to the Vimiera, for such our prize had been re-christened, in honour of the battle of that name, the news of which we had brought to the West Indies. Having taken in the powder, I proceeded to St Anne's. Two journeys on foot in a hot sun did not improve my condition; and when I returned at noon on board the Pompée, I was in a raging fever. Captain C— met me on the gangway, and reproving me for having left the ship when I felt ill, ordered me instantly into my cot. Having received the surgeon's report, he sent off for the physician of the fleet, who directed my immediate removal to the hospital. Poor Booth, the surgeon of the Pompée, escorted me there; he never again left it: he must have received the infection from me before quitting the ship, and, on reaching the quarters destined for me, he took up his own in the adjoining room.

The operation of shaving and blistering the head was performed on both; the partition that separated our apartments was not carried up to the ceiling, consequently every thing that passed in one room was distinctly audible in the other. The following evening, I was startled on perceiving Mr. Booth enter my room stark naked, and as he sat down by my bed-side, I was soon made painfully aware that reason had fled her seat. Up to this time I had not suffered my thoughts to dwell upon the probability of death, but this sudden and withering devastation of the mental and bodily powers of an immensely strong athletic man, who had been only a few hours before summoned to minister to my own sufferings and pronounce upon my fate, gave me a shock which no language can describe. I felt relieved by the entrance of the nurses and medical attendants, who with much difficulty succeeded in placing him in his bed again. The ravings of the poor maniac were terrible for many hours, when he suddenly recovered his senses, sent for the physician, Dr. Mc Arthur, and very coolly stated his last wishes, which, being committed to paper, he signed, and in a few minutes his spirit had escaped its tenement of clay. I heard his last breath; and as the passing sigh struck upon my ear, felt that it was a startling prelude to my own.

The doctor shortly came to me, when I eagerly inquired after Mr. Booth. He replied, " Oh, he is easier, much easier, and now doing well."

" Do not deceive me; he is dead, I know he is."

" Well, well, it is very true, but do not you be alarmed."

" I am not, sir, but I feel very, very ill."

The dreadful retchings with which I had been afflicted now returned with increased violence. I read my condemnation in the doctor's looks. That fatal symptom of mortality, the black vomit, had appeared—hope was extinct. In two hours more I was seized with a species of fit. The assistant surgeon put his head into the room to inquire after me: " He is just gone, sir," was the reply. At that moment my brain felt on fire; it quivered — reeled. " Good God! I am then dying!" Reason tottered on its throne, and sank for a while into the darkness of night.

When I recovered my senses, many days afterwards, I found an old black woman sitting beside me; the European lad who had attended me, and reported me as " just gone" to the surgeon, was himself a tenant of the tomb. I awoke as from a horrid dream, but with no recollection of the past. It appeared that my most vehement outcries consisted in begging the bystanders to take the gunner from me, who was thrusting a sword down my throat.

The old negress went off to report progress to the doctor, who speedily made his appearance. The care and attention of Dr. Mc Arthur is well known to those who were stationed at Barbadoes and suffered under that cruel malady. I owe much to his unwearied solicitude and skill, and though many years have elapsed, his kindness is not a whit the less vivid in my memory, or my pleasure diminished in offering this faint tribute in grateful acknowledgment of his worth.

My recovery created equal astonishment to himself and attendants; it was one of those rare instances of escape, that occur " like angels' visits, few and far between." In later years, at Jamaica, when I was captain of the guard, and making my tour of inspection round the hospital, accompanied by that excellent and much respected man Dr. Lang, I recounted the peculiarities attendant on my own case at Barbadoes.

"You may depend upon it," was his reply, "it could not have been the black vomit; recovery in such a case is quite impossible."

We entered the fever ward, and he pointed out a young lad, at the same time remarking, "There is a case of black vomit: if he were to live, I should say such an event was possible; but I have never, in that stage of the disease, seen an instance of recovery."

Singularly enough, the poor boy recovered, and Lang became a convert.

I was deplorably weak; my head, back, and chest had literally been incased in blisters. Out of the whole prize crew, consisting of thirty-four persons, Lieutenant M‒l‒d had alone escaped the fever; two seamen, another midshipman, and myself, were the sole survivors. I had been twice reported dead to Captain C— before the Pompée put to sea; but the fever having broken out with great virulence on board, she was obliged to return into port. Nearly half of the crew were attacked, but, fortunately, there were not many of them added to the frightful hecatomb of victims.

I daily recovered strength, and, soon after the restoration of my senses, was seized with an unaccountable desire to view myself in the glass. I requested the old nurse to indulge my curiosity. I found it difficult to believe that the mirror was not cheating me, as I regarded the wretched object reflected in it: my bald pate displaying the inroads of the blister cap, a countenance as yellow as a duck's foot, and the blood still oozing from eyes, ears, nose and mouth, presented altogether such a portrait of desolation as to obliterate every feature from my recollection. I burst into a flood of tears, and, like a child, wept myself asleep.

As my convalescence proceeded, I became extremely quarrelsome, and was hourly combating with my patient nurse. I insisted upon getting up.

"No, massa, you lie till to-day; doctor say him no good fo' you."

"But I will, I tell you;" and I managed to sit upright in my bed.

"You raally bery silly, for true, Massa, him tellee you lie till," and the old crone very quietly stretched her withered arm across me, and I yielded to its influence with infantine weakness.

Ere I was sufficiently re-established to leave the hospital, the apartment which had been occupied by poor Booth was tenanted by the purser of the Ringdove sloop-of-war, whose malady was general weakness. We became messmates and friends, and both were rapidly recovering, when, walking out one evening, we accidentally found ourselves in the burial-ground of the hospital. A grave was yawning ready to receive its inmate, and, just as we were leaving the enclosure, we encountered the funeral procession. We remained till the ceremony was over, but, before quitting the grave, my companion inquired the malady the deceased had died of. The usual reply, " Yellow Jack," startled the questioner, and he turned away much agitated. I was not a little surprised at the sudden change that overwhelmed him, as we had become habituated to the daily sight of victims carried to their long home.

"You are ill, L—; let us return immediately."

"I am," was his reply.

"What ails you?"

"I have caught the fever from that corpse we have just seen buried."

"Do not imagine such a thing; it is mere fancy: come, let us quicken our pace."

"It is no fancy;—to-morrow evening I shall rest there;" and turning round, he mournfully pointed to the burial-ground.

I was unable to chase away the melancholy idea that had usurped his mind; and by the time we returned to our quarters, Dr. McArthur found him in a high state of fever. He patiently submitted to all the prescriptions ordered for him, but insisted upon making his will.

Having settled his little property upon a young wife and child, he became composed and resigned. I remained with him all night. At ten o'clock the following morning he expired. His prophecy was fulfilled;—that same evening he was laid in the bosom of the earth.

Such a rapid descent from the enjoyment of life to the clammy precincts of the tomb cannot but create deeply poignant feelings in those who, enervated by previous suffering, are condemned to behold such awful instances of the instability of life. I know not what the consequences of it might have been to myself, had not Dr. Mc Arthur instantly determined upon sending me off to my ship. The society of my messmates revived my drooping spirits, but I was unable to do any duty for three months. During this time I was an inmate of the Captain's and first Lieutenant's cabins: the considerate attention of the former, and the nutritious diet he bestowed upon me, enabled me finally to surmount the serious effects attendant on attacks of extreme cases of yellow fever.

The circumstances attending poor L—'s death were certainly awful and extraordinary: he had no fear of the fever, and was in good spirits when he entered the fatal cemetery, and until the words " Yellow Jack" were pronounced, he had viewed with composure the interment of the body. Upon what metaphysical principle can we account for the sudden poisonous blight that spread itself over him? prostrating at one fell stroke the powers of mind and body, leaving him but a wreck to be tossed to and fro by the agitating impulses of a disordered imagination, and finally stranding him upon the rock which, as he had foreseen, was to silence his hopes and fears for ever. I pretend not to fathom these mysteries, or to search into the physical or moral causes that may produce such feelings and disastrous effects, resolving themselves into the word presentiment: I only know that such feelings and effects exist; and though I have witnessed similar cases, equally calamitous in their result, yet none were marked with so immediate a fulfilment of the auguries of the prescient person.

CHAPTER V.

Cruise in Fort Royal Bay, Martinique.—Successful manœuvre of the French Frigate l'Amphitrite—Recapture the Lord Cranston, a letter of marque—The late Mr. Maxwell's hospitalities—A Dignity Ball—Mulatto Beauties—Their coquetry—Nancy Clarke—Attention and kindness of Mulatto Nurses—Negroes at Bridge Town, Barbadoes—An Affray—Danger from fire of a Prize Vessel—Rejoin the Pompée—Interchange of Courtesies—Ship cleared for action—A narrow Escape—Captain P-h-ll's action with La Topaze—Melancholy occurrence—Arrival of the Expedition for the attack of Martinique—Pigeon Island reconnoitred—Explosion of a Shell—Difficult formation of a Hill-Battery—Reduction of Pigeon Island.

The ship's company recovered their health, and we took up our cruising-ground in Fort Royal Bay, Martinique, where a strict blockade was maintained, preparatory to the meditated attack upon the island. In the night we were always between Pigeon Island and Casenavire beach, receiving from each place occasionally a salute, unattended with any serious injury.

During a short absence off Point Salines, the French frigate l'Amphitrite succeeded in getting in : her captain discovered so much coolness and tact in effecting his purpose, that the manœuvre deserves to be related. He got in with the land in the night, and, knowing his enemies were cruising off Port Royal, prudently shortened sail on approaching the Diamond Rock, and stood into the bay under his topsails, where he very soon fell in with an English frigate. The Frenchman under this sail was taken for one of our own cruisers, and actually kept company with the frigate the whole night, taking care, however, to get the weather-gage without any apparent exertion on his part. The clever commander was prepared at the first peep of day to push for the carenage; and as soon as the grey light of morning streaked the horizon, clapped on every stitch of sail to work to windward, unfurling the tricolor at his peak. The English frigate, on perceiving her error, did all that could possibly be done under such circumstances; but l'Amphitrite was already under the protection of the guns of Pigeon Island when the running fight began; and the fire of Casenavire batteries, Fort Royal, and Pigeon Island, completely thwarted the strenuous endeavours of our countrymen to repair the oversight: l'Amphitrite anchored in safety. It was an annoying event, but the credit due to the Frenchman was admitted, and his conduct admired by the whole squadron.

Cruising off Point Salines, we recaptured the Lord Cranston, a rich letter of marque belonging to Liverpool, mounting twenty-six guns. She had sailed in company with a consort, the Lydia, of similar force, belonging to the same owners, but unfortunately parted company. L'Amphitrite, French frigate, which I have already mentioned, fell in with the latter, and, taking out the most valuable part of the cargo, burned her. Two days afterwards the Lord Cranston fell in with the same frigate, who was, at the time he discovered her, to leeward, with her topmasts carried away. The pugnacious propensities of the daring skipper of the Lord Cranston could not resist the temptation of trying the fortune of war with him, and he bore most gallantly down on his crippled foe; but fifty guns in a man-of-war against half that number in a merchant-vessel, soon brought the brave but unthinking Englishman to a true sense of the folly of the attempt, and, after exchanging broadsides with him at close quarters for twenty minutes, he was obliged to lower his flag to his superior enemy. It was a rash attempt, and demonstrates pretty clearly that there are cases where discretion is the better part of valour; but one cannot refrain from admiring the spirit that urged him on: a man with so much enterprise, had it been tempered with judgment, would have cut a shining figure in his Majesty's service.

The first duty I performed after quitting the hospital at Barbadoes, was conducting the Lord Cranston to Carlisle Bay: here I was detained a fortnight before the prize-agent relieved me from my charge. She was an amazingly fine vessel, and beautifully fitted up for passengers; her invoice amounted to near 100,000*l.* sterling. The French lieutenant, who had been prize-master of her, on quitting the ship, handed up so many English-looking trunks as forming part of his baggage, that I could not but suspect they had belonged to the cargo; he assured me they did not.

" But they are English: did you purchase them in France ?"

" Oh no; they form my share of the goods taken out of the Lydia."

" In that case I cannot allow you to retain them; they must be inspected."

"*Sacré nom de Dieu!*" broke from the infuriated Frenchman, " *c'est une indignité abominable!*"

I endeavoured to convince him that any intention to insult him was very foreign to my sentiments, and that I was only fulfilling a duty: that there could be no injustice on my part; for on reflection he must perceive that, as his right was obtained by capture, the fortune of war had now transferred that right to us, and we were bound to restore the goods to the original proprietors. Nothing could persuade the indignant Frenchman but that he was a most ill-treated personage, and he left me with deep-muttered threats of revenge.

The agreeable manner in which the prize-masters lived by no means excited any very anxious desire to hurry themselves in rejoining their ships. The late Mr. Maxwell kept a magnificent table and open house at his place called Passage; besides which there was a dinner at his town house every day for all those whose affairs would not permit them to leave town, and carriages and horses were ready to convey his naval friends into the country. Each prize-master was allowed ten dollars per day, and his table was abundantly supplied with the good things of this life : it was a style of independence and luxury unsuited to the wild schemes and thoughtless extravagance of Middies. I little dreamed that I was afterwards to pay so high a price for all these superlative delights.

For the first time, I attended with my brother reefers a Dignity ball, very properly so denominated. The female portion of the company was composed of Mulatto girls, dressed out in the first style of the last-imported fashions from Europe. The stateliness and dignity assumed by these ladies on being introduced to them were laughable. No pale cold beauty of the North could require more assiduous attention and respect to induce them to enter into familiar discourse, than did these dark houries of the Tropics. The slightest freedom (before the period deemed decorous in their opinion to descend from their high stilts) was instantly met by, " Good Goramity ! why, what you tak me for? you no hab court me yet: you raally too free, sar." Dancing is their heaven, although they do not exhibit the animation which their devotion to it would lead us to expect. Dignity, dignity, restrains them from giving loose to their natural inclinations. The attention they exact from those who would stand high in their favour is ridiculous; and at the time I am writing of, the assemblage of military and naval officers being greater than usual, their consequence increased in proportion to the number of admirers buzzing around them. Indeed, he was considered fortunate who could obtain a partner, and it was only by the most obsequious gallantry and flowery compliments that he was permitted to retain his seat by his charmer.*

Nancy Clarke, that well known-purveyor of all that was good, and whose house might be looked

* I had made an attempt to describe one of these assemblies at my old friend Betsy Austin's; but a like scene, inimitably and correctly portrayed by the amusing "Peter Simple," has thrown my own so far into the shade that I feel it wise to abstain from presenting it to the notice of my readers.—"I come here for dance, sar, and not for chatter," conveyed me at once into the presence of the Misses Eurydice, Aspasia, and Co. tripping it on the light fantastic toe under the guidance of that Prince of Mulatto musicians, Massa Apollo Johnson, whose well *turned* leg and appendant foot form the *beau idéal* of negro symmetry.

upon as the head-quarters of his Majesty's naval subjects, still continued her hospitable attentions and womanly care of those inmates who placed themselves under her roof. The expenses certainly were heavy, but there was so much of motherly kindness and good humour about the old lady, that we felt more gratification in paying her bills than would have been experienced in handing half the same amount to another hostess. If an unfortunate reefer found his funds running low, and stated the fact to the good old girl as an excuse for not rubbing off the score, her remark of " Nebber mind, my son, anoder time all de same ting;—here, you boy,—you no hear 'em verree; go bring glass of sangaree for Massa," would finish the colloquy. I should say from what I have heard and witnessed, few tavern-keepers (if any) were ever less plagued with bad debts than Nancy Clarke; she thrived accordingly, and died, as I understand, very rich. Her most anxious thoughts were directed towards the education of her daughter; she procured her every advantage that money could bestow. I have never heard whether the girl responded to all these maternal cares, but the fact certainly places poor Nancy in an amiable point of view. The universal estimation in which this excellent creature was held, was manifested on her arrival at Portsmouth by all ranks in the navy, from the Port-Admiral to the youngest commissioned officer who had benefited by her attentions. Had she been Queen of the Indies, it would have been difficult to have heaped more civilities upon her. Admirals, Colonels, Commissioners, Captains, and Commanders, were seen in her train, as she was escorted round the dock-yard, garrison, &c. The simplicity of Nancy caused no little amusement, and some embarrassment, when, on being introduced to the family of an old officer, and the younger branches being ushered in for admiration, she exclaimed with the utmost *naïveté*, pointing to the youngest child, " Good Goramity! how like your lily boy to your son George at Barbadoes,"—thereby recalling most inopportunely to his recollection the inadvertencies of his younger days, in the presence of his fair lady, whose correct ideas were shocked at this public exposure of her husband's juvenile indiscretions.

The attention and kindness of the mulatto women to Europeans when sick, are beyond all praise. Naturally of an indolent disposition, they freely indulge in it; but when once they take upon themselves the charge of a sick person, (and they will not do it unless they feel interested for you,) no beings can exert themselves more diligently and faithfully in the discharge of their duties, anticipating every wish and want, and watching over you with all the solicitude and interest of a dear friend. I am sure I owe my life to one of these excellent creatures,—my friend Loretta, at Port Royal, in 1826, when I was again attacked with Yellow Jack. I lodged in her house, which was close to the hospital. She concocted a preparation of her own, composed of lime-juice, eau de Cologne, and other medicaments, with which she ever and anon sponged my body. It was perfect elysium to my fevered senses, but was kept a profound secret from the medical men who attended me. Had I not been under a strict promise to the kind Loretta to be silent on the subject, I could scarcely have refrained from communicating a recipe from which I fancied I had received more benefit than from all the doctor's drugs. At night she lay on a sofa in my room, and so great was her watchfulness, that if I moved she was up in an instant, and I was soothed to rest again by the magical effects of her prescription.

The novelty of having a boat at my command frequently led me, in company with the other prize-masters, to visit the shore. The negroes at Bridge Town, Barbadoes, are noted as the most impudent of their race throughout the West Indies; their accuracy in throwing stones is proverbial, and sometimes disagreeably displayed. Returning one evening to our boat in the bay, some of these black idlers, without any provocation, let fly a volley of stones at us, one of which struck me a severe blow on the elbow. We instantly gave chase, but only arrived at the corner of the street in time to see the retreating form of one of them enter a house. Finding the door locked, we scaled the window, and got into the court, where Mr. Blacky, having possessed himself of his master's fowling-piece, defended the head of the stairs. Levelling the gun, he called out most lustily, " So elp me Goramity, massa, pose you come here, me shootee you." Being unarmed, we wisely desisted, and made our retreat as we had entered. The triumph of the niggers could not be controlled; they hung upon our flanks, and we were saluted as we were stepping into our boat with another volley. By a skilful manœuvre on our part the *blackguards* were separated, and my friend blacky with the fowling-piece, finding himself cut off in his retreat, took shelter in the shell of a house building on the beach. Here I followed my gentleman, and the fellow again levelled the piece within three feet of my head, jabbering and showing his ivories like a frightened monkey. But our positions were now altered; I was armed with a good stretcher, and my antagonist pinned to the wall. With my left hand I turned the muzzle on one side, and with the other aiming a well-directed blow on his thick noddle, succeeded in disarming and making him prisoner. On inspecting the gun it was found to be loaded with small shot, primed, and cocked. I was only astonished it had not gone off in the fright of the culprit. What was to be done with the fellow? I proposed conveying him on board, and giving him a sound flogging: but the strict island laws respecting carrying off slaves alarmed my companions, and the fellow was allowed to depart, though not *Scot free.* Fifty yards were measured off, and being given that distance for a start, the contents of the fusil were sent after him, and tickled his back in a greater degree than he found at all pleasant.

It was a propitious event for myself, and for the Martinique expedition at that time assembling in Carlisle Bay, (and of course proportionally unfortunate for the garrison of that island,) that I was not longer detained with my negro friend on shore.

On reaching the prize, which was anchored in the midst of the transports preparing for the enterprise, I was surprised at not being hailed, and absolutely astounded when, on mounting the side, I found no one on deck. My astonishment was mingled with serious alarm on observing a volume of smoke issuing from the companion ladder. I darted down into the cabin, from which I was obliged to make a hasty retreat, being nearly suffocated by the thick smoke that filled the apartment; but not before I had aroused the mate of the vessel, and my second in command, who were both lying fast asleep on sofas, unconscious of the impending danger. The boat's crew had, in the mean time, drawn water. The fire, as I ascended to the deck, broke out from under the ladder of the bulk-head; before it was fairly ignited, a plentiful supply of water stopped the progress of the flames, and, by following up our advantage, it was happily mastered. A few minutes later, and her fate would have been inevitable; and from the dead calm that then reigned, many of the surrounding vessels would have doubtless shared in the calamity. It is impossible to calculate upon the extent of mischief that must have ensued among such a mass of vessels as were there congregated.

The fire originated from the unpardonable breach of orders, carelessness, and downright stupidity of the steward, who, when drawing off some rum, stuck the candle against the bulk-head, which circumstance he had forgotten. The candle soon fell between the rum cask and the bulk-head among a quantity of loose birch, which taking fire, speedily communicated itself to the cask and bulk-head. So near were we to destruction, that when the fire was totally extinguished, on examining the rum cask, one part of it had been so burned through, that, on the pressure of the finger against the charred part, it passed at once into the vessel, and set the liquor flowing. Had the rum once ignited, it would have spread like liquid fire in the hold, and nothing could have saved us.

The deplorable loss of the Kent East Indiaman originated from a similar cause; and there is too much reason to fear that a want of requisite caution on board merchant-vessels may have contributed to the destruction of many of those of which no tidings have been received. The strict enforcement of the regulations respecting fire and lights on board his Majesty's ships forbids the remotest chance of such an accident. It appears a species of madness on the part of men possessed of common sense, to think of so dangerous an attempt in a ship's hold by candle-light. I should almost as soon think of taking a naked light into the magazine.

This serious misadventure made me apply earnestly next morning to the agent, to relieve me of my charge, and allow me to proceed by the

York, which was then preparing to get under weigh to join the Pompée. I succeeded in having the responsibility taken off my shoulders, and lost not a moment in going on board of her. It required some time to elapse before I could reflect upon our narrow escape without trembling, for I had undoubtedly no business to be away from her at that hour of the night.

The Pompée had resumed her station in Port Royal Bay, Martinique, and I was installed as signal officer. The day after I had rejoined her, we took a French cutter from France, on board of which was a large quantity of every description of stock belonging to the governor Villaret Joyeuse, despatched from his own estate in Normandy. Captain C— immediately desired the governor's stock and personal property to be valued, and, paying over the amount of them to the agent, sent the whole in with a flag-of-truce to his Excellency. Such a mark of attention could not fail to have its due effect, and a letter of thanks, expressing the highest gratification, accompanied by a present of rich liqueurs and noyau, acknowledged the handsome conduct of his gallant foe. It is by such interchange of courtesies among noble spirits that the narrow prejudices of personal animosity are swept away; for they lead to that chivalrous feeling between contending foes, which ennobles human nature amidst the sanguinary contests of the battle-field, and tends to soften the asperities of actual warfare.

The arrival of one French frigate, and the knowledge of others having quitted Europe for the express purpose of throwing in supplies to the strictly blockaded island, kept us constantly on the alert. The report of two large sail seen to leeward sent the old Pompée in chase, and the signal officer to the mast-head to reconnoitre the strangers. The first that came within the field of my telescope was so completely English, that I reported at once two English frigates. My cursory glance deserved rebuke. When their upper sails were first seen from the deck, the Captain's glass fell upon the sternmost: he instantly turned round to me, saying—

"Do you call those English-cut sails, sir?"

I acknowledged I had only examined the headmost, and received my deserts.

On the first report of their being in sight we had made all sail, and, as we approached the strangers on an angle with their course, we quickly came within signal distance. The private signal was hoisted, but no answer returned, and we cleared ship for action; the guns were reloaded and double-shotted. The evening waxed late; we fancied they kept more away, and were endeavouring to avoid us. Two bells in the first watch had struck, the private signal for the night had been twice repeated, without acknowledgment.

"They are enemies,—not a doubt of it," was whispered from one to the other; "who could have thought otherwise?"

Captain C— immediately determined upon the adoption of decided measures to prevent the possibility of their escape. The unfortunate one astern was destined to receive the whole of our broadside, which, if it did not send her to the bottom, must have so crippled her, that she must at once have been placed *hors du combat*, and we were then to pass on to secure the headmost.

The captains of the guns stood with the laniards of the locks in their hands, as we ranged up abeam of the sternmost frigate: when so close that our yard-arms nearly projected over each other, the Captain hailed her—

" What ship is that?"

" This is the French frigate La Topaze,"—was all we heard.

" Stand by!" repeated our chief, and the arms of all the captains of the guns were simultaneously raised. One untoward jerk, or had one gun gone off by accident after closing him, the whole broadside would have been poured on her decks; fortunately, our commanding officer was calm and self-possessed, so that before he issued the fatal command ' Fire!' he asked—

" Is she a captured ship?"

" Prize to the Cleopatra ahead;"—and the hopes of a fight, prizes, and prize-money, quickly resolved themselves into nothing.

We passed on to the Cleopatra, and Captain P–h–ll soon made his appearance on board. Captain C—'s devotion to the welfare of the service led him to spare no man, however high might be the rank, or conspicuous the abilities of the person meriting reproof; and his vexation at having been drawn far to leeward of an important point, thereby leaving it unguarded and accessible to the entrée of the enemy's vessels, was a sufficient cause of irritation to one who was rigidly faithful and strict in the discharge of his duty: his feelings may therefore be supposed to have been anything but mollified at finding " *qu'il avait couru après la lune*," and found only the shadow just as he had believed himself secure of the substance. But if the gallant officer who had then so lately distinguished himself by the capture of La Topaze, did meet with a reproof, owing to the unfortunate circumstance of his having for a time mislaid the private signals, and not having stood towards us when he found we were English; annoying as it must have been for the moment, he doubtless placed the reproof to its true source, originating on the part of the superior officer from exceeding anxiety to adhere to the duties prescribed by the service; and, as such, he must have naturally dismissed it from his mind. I afterwards understood that, on the preceding night, Captain P–h–ll, having occasion to refer to the private signals when in his cot, had slipped them under his pillow instead of returning them into the box kept for that purpose, as was his usual habit. In the morning the cot was of course lashed up, and the signals were not thought of again until they fell in with us, when they were not to be found, his disposal of them in the night having quite escaped his memory.

It only shows in what jeopardy we may be sometimes placed even by our friends, though belonging to the best-regulated ships in the service.

Captain P–h–ll's action with La Topaze was marked by peculiar judgment and ability. In company with the Hazard he came upon the enemy, who was at anchor at Point Noire, Guadaloupe, under the protection of a battery on shore, while he was busily employed discharging a quantity of flour and landing troops, having given up the hope of succeeding in getting it and them to their destination, Martinique. In the hurry of getting ready for action, the Frenchman had cleared away that side of the deck opposed to his enemies, in doing which he lumbered up the other next the shore. The manner in which he had evidently been employed did not escape the penetration of Captain P–h–ll, who, following the example of Nelson at the Nile, ran alongside of the enemy in shore, shot away his spring, and took the unfortunate Frenchman at an advantage he had not foreseen: before he could get his guns to bear, the fire of his adversary had deprived him of the hope of successfully prolonging the contest. The arrival of the Jason settled the business, and the gallant Captain of the Cleopatra had the gratification of reaping the fruits of his instant decision and correct judgment, by conducting La Topaze to the Commander-in-chief. While pursuing his course for this purpose we fell in with him. Fortunately, the melancholy effects that might have occurred from our meeting, were avoided by the cool and steady conduct of the Pompée's chief; otherwise, the very circumstance which was a source of honour to Captain P–h–ll, and of pride to his brother officers, might have turned out a never-failing subject of poignant regret, as leading to a catastrophe which would have been for ever deeply deplored.

A melancholy occurrence took place off St. Pierre at this period. The Morne Fortunée, a small brig commanded by a lieutenant, stationed off the town, was directly to leeward of the island, and the water smooth as a mill pond, when a sudden squall, arising from the land, is supposed to have taken her aback, and sent her down stern foremost. Out of a crew of nearly seventy men, the only beings saved were a master's mate and the crew of a boat that had been sent in-shore to attack a small craft, two or three of whom, with the master's mate, were wounded before they got clear off with her: not a vestige of the wreck of the Morne Fortunée was ever discovered.

The anxiously looked for expedition for the attack of Martinique at length arrived. A landing, under the able management of Capt. Beaver, was immediately effected without opposition in Cul de Sac Robert; followed, on the part of the enemy, by the destruction of the Carnation, which had been captured by them, and had taken refuge in the neighbouring harbour of Marin. On the same evening the small battery on Pointe Solomon was stormed and taken by the York Rangers and blue-jackets.

Our captain, accompanied by Sir Charles Shipley, hastened to reconnoitre the immediate environs of Pigeon Island, below which that part of the squadron under Capt. C— was anchored out of gun-shot. A projecting rock on the mainland, about long musket-shot from Pigeon Island, was fixed upon as a good situation for a mortar. The materials for forming the platform, &c. were immediately prepared; and as soon as night closed in to shelter us from the view of the enemy, the boats moved forward in silence to the spot, where with great difficulty a thirteen-inch mortar was landed, without drawing upon us the attention of the enemy; and at daylight Johnny was astonished at being saluted from such close quarters by a shell that was plumped into the centre of the little fort.

The rocks, forming a natural parapet, protected this our first battery from the fire of the enemy's guns; and the spot itself was so small, that not one shell fell into it, though the whole force of Pigeon Island, at least all that could be brought to bear, was instantly directed against it. In approaching and retiring from this advanced position, the boats were sufficiently skreened from the view of the besieged, and were comparatively safe from shot, though the outside oars, being exposed, were repeatedly shot away by the guns.

It was of material consequence that the reduction of this fort should be effected as speedily as possible, in order to give us the command of the bay; and the battery being found insufficient, Sir C. Shipley and Capt. C— proceeded to seek out a spot upon which a more formidable one might be erected. This was, from the face of the surrounding country, a task of considerable difficulty; the land towards Pigeon Island being almost perpendicular. At a hundred paces in rear of the mortar we had already planted, was the entrance to a valley, but so precipitous in its ascent and descent, as almost to equal the nearly perpendicular cliff which looked towards the enemy's fort. With no small toil, the engineer and his companions gained the summit of the mount called Morne Vanier, which completely overlooked the enemy. This spot had been surveyed by a French engineer, and was reported inaccessible to the formation of a battery: it was consequently left unprotected, and we took possession of it.

"No spot could be better adapted for our purpose,"—so Sir Charles Shipley expressed himself; but at the same time he declared he saw no practicable method by which the guns could be brought up, and pronounced the execution of the plan as next to impossible.

"If you fix upon this spot," was our Captain's reply, "I will be answerable that in two days the guns shall be placed here."

"I fear it is impracticable," replied the Engineer; "but, could it be managed, the enemy would be unable to hold out twelve hours after its completion."

"In that case I undertake to arrange every thing according to your wishes, and in two days the necessary complement of mortars and howitzers shall be mounted."—Captain C—'s comprehensive mind had at once embraced all the difficulties, and their remedy; and they returned on board to issue the requisite directions. I was immediately despatched in the barge with the carpenters to commence cutting away the trees at the bottom of the hill, and those that grew from the insterstices of the rocky mountain to the top.

I had scarcely landed when the Frenchmen, beginning to suspect that such might be the case, threw a thirteen-inch shell over the hill, which, passing close above our heads, struck the opposite side of the narrow part of the valley where we were standing, and rolled down amongst us. The whole of the men, with the exception of two carpenters and myself, lay down to wait its explosion. I had not then formed so intimate an acquaintance with those shin-breakers as afterwards fell to my lot; fancying the danger past, I addressed the men, "What the devil are you all lying down for, you fools?" The coxswain of the barge, an old quarter-master, replied in his gruff seaman's tone, "By G—, sir, if you are wise you'll lie down also." As he finished the sentence, the shell exploded, and one of the splinters carried off both the legs above the knees of the poor fellows who were standing beside me; I remained unhurt not a foot distant from the sufferers. We instantly applied our handkerchiefs as *tourniquets*, and succeeded in stopping the terrible effusion of blood: they were immediately sent off to the ship, but they both expired before the boat reached her.

I profited by that morning's melancholy lesson ever afterwards: when a shell fell disagreeably near me, I failed not to recollect the old quartermaster's advice, and instantly prostrated myself at full length in a line with my unwelcome neighbour, patiently awaiting in that respectful position the explosion of its rage.

A strong reinforcement soon arrived with our Captain, who superintended the operations, and was ably seconded by Captain F. Collier, of His Majesty's ship Circe. The valley was alive with the busy hum of two-hundred blue-jackets and marines, and the stroke of the axe and the tomahawk resounded far and wide; giant trees and modest shrubs alike fell beneath the sturdy blows of the intruders. Before Nature hid her face in the mantle of night, the timber was cleared away to the summit, and the nearly perpendicular and projecting rocks were shorn of the entangled lofty shade that had for ages clothed their rugged sides. The stream cable was then secured at the summit, and conducted down the hill as straight as the irregularities of the ground would permit. Luff tackles, and small hawsers, were deposited on the projecting masses of rock, which served as resting-places. Every man was furnished with a canvass belt, fitted with a toggle.

All necessary arrangements being made, a messenger was despatched before daybreak to the ordnance transports, to say we were waiting for the howitzers and mortars. On their arrival, our indefatigable Captain, who, if he worked us hard, did not spare himself, appeared determined not to exceed the time he had allotted himself for the fulfilment of his engagement. While these operations were expeditiously carrying on by us, the engineers were not less vigorous in their department, and were assisted by the working-party in raising the parapets, laying the platforms, constructing the magazine, &c.

The French kept up a constant, but not well-directed fire of shells; indeed, as we were working in a line with the parabola of their descent, the difficulty of annoying us was great, except at the bottom of the valley, or by breaking them over our heads, in which they seldom succeeded. The casualties were therefore singularly few, considering so many busy bees were congregated together in so small a space, and these chiefly occurred from the few shells which did explode in the air; either their fuses were bad, or there was great want of judgment in cutting them.

By the time the party had breakfasted, the first mortar had arrived; stages were ready to land them, and soon the heaviest, a thirteen-incher, was at the foot of the declivity. The single blocks of the luff tackles were hooked on to the selvagees attached to the stream cable, the other hook to the chain round the trunnions of the mortar, and the fall led upwards: small hawsers were led down on each side the stream-cable as man ropes, by which the seamen were to haul themselves up. Everything being ready, the men, with their canvass belts passed over one shoulder, clapped on their toggles to the tackle falls; their arms being thus left at full liberty, they drew themselves and the mortar after them up the steep, landing it here and there on the projecting ledges of the rock. By these simple means, apparently insuperable difficulties were overcome, and all the pieces were in battery before sunset without a single accident, except those arising from the fire of the enemy. Captain C— accomplished his task within twelve hours of the stated period.

I should be almost afraid to specify the quantity of swizzle individually made away with during the six-and-thirty hours we were thus employed. But nature was so heavily taxed as to have required it; our continued exertions drew forth such copious streams of perspiration, that ever and anon I was obliged to wring the cuffs of my light jacket, as if they had been steeped in a brook. The completion of this difficult job is a convincing proof of the powers of Englishmen, when directed by a skilful commander, encouraging them in his own person, by partaking in an equal or greater degree the fatigues and dangers of the enterprise. There are few men whose constitutions would enable them to undergo greater or severer fatigue than Capt. C— always imposed upon himself when the welfare or benefit of the service was concerned: his unbounded zeal in face of an enemy never allowed him to feel weary, or want of rest to oppress him; and he could not suppose others to be differently affected.

Impossible, was a word on these occasions erased from his vocabulary.

In the course of the night the necessary quantity of shells and powder was carried up, and the battery completed at all points. At daybreak the intervening shrubs and underwood that masked it from the view of the enemy were cleared away, and the howitzers and mortar ready to open their fire as soon as the objects became distinctly visible.

The mortar which had been first planted had sadly annoyed the little garrison, but when the hill battery commenced on the 3rd February, they were literally pounded into submission. In three hours the white flag was hoisted; but, not agreeing to the terms proposed, they had a few hours more of the same severe regimen, which induced them to surrender at discretion.

This rapid and brilliant success so gratified the Commander-in-chief, that, immediately after the reduction of Pigeon Island, Captain C— was ordered to hoist a Commodore's broad pendant, and Captain P. Brenton was appointed his captain.

CHAPTER VI.

Lieutenant-General Beckwith's decided action.—Take possession of Fort Royal.—Erection of Batteries.—An Accident.—Loss of life during the construction of the Sailors' Battery.—Manœuvres to avoid the Shells.—Conveying the Guns to the Battery.—Mulatto Girls.—A dangerous Adventure.—Cool and intrepid conduct of Captain S—th of the Engineers.—The Batteries completed.—The Bombardment.—The Enemy's sally repulsed.—Merit neglected.—A Truce.—Hostilities recommenced.—The Author wounded.—Kindness of his messmates.—He is removed on board.—Surrender of Fort Bourbon.—Author visits the Fort.—The captive Garrison embarked.—Court Martial on the Officers and Men of the Carnation.—The Sentence.—Reflections.—The Execution.

THE decided action of Lieutenant-General Beckwith with the whole of the enemy's forces on Mount Sourière, made them abandon all farther open resistance, and they shut themselves up in Forts Royal and Bourbon. The night previous to the surrender of Pigeon Island, two of our frigates, the Cleopatra and Æolus, with the Recruit brig, pushed up to the head of the bay in gallant style, under a heavy fire from Negro Point and Pigeon Island, so that all escape for the garrison was completely cut off, supposing any attempt should be made from Fort Royal with that intention. This movement was followed by the enemy's abandoning Fort Royal, or Edward, and setting fire to the Amphitrite French frigate. Captain Napier, of the Recruit, in the course of the day landed at the fort with only a boat's crew, mounted the ramparts, and having ascertained the desertion of the enemy, immediately communicated the fact to the Commander-in-chief.

The enemy, fearful of dividing their force, abandoned all the batteries along Casenavire beach and Fort Royal, in order to concentrate their strength in Fort Bourbon.* After re-embarking all our stores and ordnance, we proceeded to the opposite side of the bay. The whole of the naval force intended to co-operate with the army had landed at Negro Point, where the Commodore

* Fort Dessaix.

took up his head-quarters in the evening. In consequence of Captain Napier's dashing *reconnaissance*, a strong party of the York Rangers embarked in the boats and proceeded to take possession of Fort Royal, where they secured themselves from any sudden attack of the enemy, and, throwing up a breastwork in the body of the place, planted some of the guns against their late owners in Fort Bourbon. As daylight dawned, it discovered to them the British flag flying upon the walls. It appears that the commanding height of Fort Bourbon, or Dessaix, as it had been re-christened, led the French to believe that it would have proved no difficult matter to drive us out should we attempt to take possession of it; but they did not calculate upon our being enabled to transform it into a mischievous battery against themselves.

No time was lost in landing all the stores requisite for the immediate erection of the different batteries against the fortress. The Intrepid, sixty-four, got out her lower-deck guns, (twenty-four pounders,) for the sailors' batteries. A zig-zag road was cut through a wood to the spot, and Mount Tartanson fixed upon as the principal mortar battery: it was speedily constructed by the blue-jackets, who were principally employed on that side the fort. The battery was completed and armed without the French discovering us : which they did in consequence of a melancholy accident taking place the morning of its completion. A tent, containing a large quantity of powder and combustibles, by some unaccountable accident (which never was explained) blew up, killing and wounding several of our men. Fortunately the greater number of the working-party had commenced their return to the encampment, or the list of sufferers would in all probability have been frightfully swelled.

The next work to be constructed was the sailors' battery to the left of the mortar just completed. Here we were discovered before we began to break ground, and the flight of shot and shell was uninterrupted. The site of the encampment of the troops on this side the fort, near the sailors' quarters, though hidden from the view of the enemy, appeared to be pretty correctly known, if we might judge from the number of twenty-four pounders and thirteen-inch shells that were daily and nightly thrown into it. The average loss of men might be computed from eight to ten each night. The mischief caused by the twenty-four pounders was speedily obviated by the erection of a parapet, but there was no combating with the destructive effect of the shells. Most of the poor fellows thus carried off passed from a sound refreshing sleep, secured to them by the fatigues of the day, into that of eternity.

Men speedily become familiarized with death and danger, and though we knew the shells would break in upon our slumbers, silencing for ever the heavy breathing of some poor tired unconscious being, I do not think that on this account we slept a jot the less soundly upon our earthy beds, or envied those who were pillowed on down: extreme corporeal exertion overpowered other feelings, and rendered us insensible to harassing reflections; we were only too happy to seek our rude couch and resign ourselves to an uncertain state of repose.

It frequently happened that in proceeding to the sailors' battery we were obliged to prostrate ourselves to the fallen shells,—a sort of *faccia in terra* manœuvre, so particularly recommended by

Italian bandits as preventive of evil consequences to those unlucky wights who fall in their way. Whether I should pay the same quantum of respect to the behests of the aforesaid imperious gentlemen, would depend upon circumstances, but there is no disputing my sedulous attention to the movement, or my desire to avoid the heavy penalty attending any neglect of such prostration by the explosion of these angry messengers. " Practice makes perfect," and I latterly became extremely expert in the necessary evolutions, and used to watch and dodge the descent of a shell with much nicety and exactitude. The cry of " Shell! shell!—down! down!" was decisive; and down dropped every soul at full length— *n'importe*, puddle, mud, or mire; we were not at all dainty upon such occasions. When heavy rain had fallen, those nearest to the bomb were nearly suffocated by the shower of dirt, &c. spattered over them by its explosion. This was the signal for a *levée en masse*, and, should our party have escaped uninjured, the roars of laughter excited by the ludicrous figures we exhibited, bedaubed and bespotted from head to foot with mud, impeded our yoking-to again till another iron messenger would stop our mirth, and remind us of our folly in remaining longer exposed to danger. It was ridiculous enough to observe in open spaces the awkward attempts of a party to avoid the shell when seen in mid air and directed towards them; every eye would be fixed upon the projectile, first running forwards, and then as instantly back again, some to the right, others to the left, staggering, stumbling, and knocking one another over, from their eyes being directed upwards, till the moment of its fall, when down they would all drop as if they had been shot. As the shell buries itself deep in the earth, on its explosion the splinters fly off, from the equal resistance of all around, something in the line of a semicircle: if therefore you can get within ten or twelve feet of it, lying flat in a direction with the shell, you are comparatively safe.

In one of these trips to the battery, a seaman, in endeavouring to escape from a thirteen-inch shell, which he observed descending, ran forward, as if it had been his fate, to the very spot of its fall: it appeared to explode at the instant it impinged his person, and literally blew him to atoms.

Notwithstanding the annoyance and destruction caused by the enemy's fire, the sailors' battery was soon formed and ready for the guns. In transporting them there we had to cross the road from St. Pierre to Fort Royal, in diverging from which we were for a short space exposed to the full view of Fort Bourbon, and they were always prepared to give us a *salvo*. On arriving at this spot we generally halted for a rest preparatory to a rally. Thus recruited, we started off as fast as the twenty-four pounder at our tail would permit us. In turning the corner, the leading men not taking a sufficient sweep, the wheels of the limber to which the gun was slung slipped off the road, and down went the whole concern into the ditch, exactly in the spot where we were most exposed to the fire of the fort.

Whether it proceeded from anxiety or hurry on the part of the French, or whether our good genius was then in the ascendant, it is not for me to determine; but though we were detained in extricating the piece upwards of an hour, it so happened that not a single man was killed or wounded, although the fire was incessant. When clear of the dangerous spot, and under the shelter of a wood, a chance shot passed through and carried off two of our party. *Telle est la fortune de la guerre.*

During the day our little encampment was visited by the mulatto girls, who brought us eggs, vegetables, and other refreshments. I cannot positively declare at this distance of time whether a laudable anxiety to procure more substantial delicacies for the palates of my messmates, or an indescribable *je ne sais quoi* lurking in the eyes of one of these dark houries, prompted me, after the fatiguing duties of the day, to volunteer my services on a foraging expedition in the immediate vicinity of the beleaguered enemy. The master of the bewitching dark one was a French militia Colonel, who (looking to the interests of number one after Lieutenant-General Beckwith's action on the heights above Bourbon, and seeing the utter hopelessness of his countrymen holding out,) had seceded from the governor and garrison, and secretly came over to us, communicating all the intelligence worthy of notice.

His house was situated just above the town of Fort Royal, to the left of the road leading up to Fort Bourbon, and on the declivity of the hill, upon the summit of which rested the fortress. The Colonel's mansion, though completely under its guns, was betwixt the two lines of fire directed towards the besiegers' batteries. Between this spot and our lines a deep valley intervened, which might be regarded as neutral ground.

Without reflecting on the length of time to which my visit might be prolonged, I started off without knowing either the parole or countersign for the night. It was one of those beautiful evenings when all nature lies hushed in deep repose, and every living thing rests in peace except the destroyer man. The outline of the form of the watchful sentinel pacing the lofty ramparts, as he uttered the "*Qui vive?*" might be clearly traced in relief against the sky. Not a sound broke in upon the scene, except the explosional discharge of a gun from the enemy, or a mortar, whose messenger might be distinctly seen, like a meteor in heaven's vast concave, pursuing its destructive course.

I had crossed the valley, and was within a few paces of the Colonel's habitation, when the challenge of the French sentries sounded so uncomfortably close, that I began to think discretion would be my better course; and I had half turned round with the intention of retiring, when the jests of my companions at " marching up the hill and down again" rose unpleasantly vivid before me, and I at once abandoned the wiser plan, and, knocking gently at the door of the gallant Colonel, was ushered in an unexpected guest. I succeeded in the ostensible object of my visit, and passed away two or three hours most agreeably with the ladies of the family. I then took my leave, and had nearly gained the brow of the hill leading down into the valley, when a sudden rush from some low trees close in my front made me clap my hand upon my sword. The sight of a horseman, and the challenge of " *Qui vive?*" did not relieve my apprehensions that I was entrapped; but, observing only one adversary, I determined to make an attempt to gain the brow, and, once there, I fancied my retreat secure. " *Qui vive?*" uttered again in a sharp tone, induced me to answer "*Un ami*," and, sidling up to the cavalier, I was on the point of proving myself anything but what I had just announced, by making a desperate blow at him with my sabre, and bolting headlong down the valley, when my hostile intentions were defeated by the good-humoured laugh of our friend the militia Colonel, replying, "*Ah, c'est vous, Monsieur S——. Diable, que faites vous ici!*" The explanation was short, and I pursued my way with double-quick but cautious steps, having learned that the French patrole was between me and our lines.

The idea of being made prisoner upon an excursion prompted solely by the indulgence of a silly whim was something so unofficerlike, and must have been considered so improper when the truth should be known, that I inwardly cursed my folly fifty times before I found myself a prisoner to our own advanced posts, where I was very properly detained, being unable to give the parole or countersign. The field-officer relieved me from my thraldom, when, instead of retiring to rest, I had to join my party towards the sailors' battery, too well contented at my escape, and blessing my good fortune that I had not shared the fate of two other officers, who, it appeared, had marched off upon a similar expedition in the very same quarter, and upon whom the enemy's patrole stumbled. They were conducted to Fort Bourbon, where they remained in an unenviable state of mind: fired at by their countrymen, with the risk every moment of mutilation or death dealt by the hands of friends. It cured me of my wandering propensities.

The sailors' battery, consisting of nine twenty-four pounders, two mortars, and three eight-inch howitzers, being completed, a smaller one was commenced to the left of that again. The army under Lieutenant-General Beckwith had of course completely invested the fort, and were as busily employed as we were. Another party of seamen, under the command of Captain Barton, were likewise busily engaged at the head of the bay.

The admiration of the blue-jackets was greatly excited by the cool conduct of Captain Charles S—th of the Engineers, and the contempt of danger he at all times displayed. This officer was appointed to superintend the construction of the batteries to which the seamen were attached, and to direct their labours: we could not but admire his imperturbable equanimity. I felt highly amused at watching him one day eating his dinner. Descending from the parapet, where he had been exposed all the morning to a hot fire, he quietly seated himself upon the ground a little to the right of the battery, and, placing the plate upon his knees, began a vigorous attack upon the savoury viands. The second mouthful was on its way when a twenty-four pound shot grazed so close to him that it scattered the earth over himself and his dinner. The plate being cleared of this unwelcome condiment, he again set-to, in no way ruffled in temper or disposed to balk his appetite. A second ball played him the same malicious trick, when he got up and removed himself, his dinner, and his three bottles of porter, behind the parapet, and, once more settling his affairs, he exclaimed "Now fire away and be d—d to you!" Five minutes had perhaps elapsed, when, as he was quaffing off a draught of porter, a shell fell in his rear, and, exploding, covered him with dirt and buried the remains of his luckless dinner. I think I see him now rising and shaking the rubbish from his shoulders, his patience at length exhausted by the loss of his repast, and in irritated accents apostrophizing the inconsiderate Frenchmen with " D—n your eyes, master Johnny, can't you let me have my dinner in peace ?"

On the 17th of February 1809, the Commodore had completed, with the naval brigade, the three batteries entrusted to his erection. In two days more, those on the opposite side were ready, and the 19th, at three o'clock in the afternoon, was the appointed time for the opening salute. The Commodore was to give the preparatory signal to the other batteries by firing one gun and displaying his broad pendant at the sailors' battery.

At two o'clock, the first party who had the honour to man the guns, headed by the Commodore, marched up a few minutes before the stated time in high glee, to pay off the score the enemy had been running up in our books. It had been a sad annoyance to Jack to be fired at by those " thundering Frenchmen" without being able to give a single shot in return ; but now he observed, " It is our turn, and if we don't touch him off to the nines, why, as Jonathan says, 'there's no snakes in Virginia.'"

The embrasures were unmasked, and at the prescribed moment bang went one of the twenty-four pounders,* and the swallow-tailed flag proudly fluttered over our heads. The next shot was the signal to commence, and in one instant the din and roar of shot and shell from all quarters was stunning. The besieged appeared determined to keep pace with us; their fire was well kept up, and the accuracy with which they dropped their shells into our battery obliged us now and then to discontinue the fire of some of our pieces to repair our embrasures and parapets. For four hours the discharge was uninterrupted, when the guns became so heated that we were forced to slacken our fire; but we were preceded in this necessary act by the Frenchmen. The animation of our chief, and the inspiring applause he bestowed upon our exertions, communicated to us fresh ardour and vigour: the broad pendant was perforated to rags.

* Thirty-one mortars and twenty-four twenty-pounders were opened upon the fort.

Ere ten o'clock had arrived, the contending parties appeared fatigued with this first display of their mutual strength : the tremendous fire sustained for many hours dwindled into the discharge of a single shot and shell, at intervals of five or six minutes, like the growlings of a retiring thunder-storm. Our loss in killed and wounded was trifling. It was now our turn to be relieved, having had a spell of seven hours' hard work. We slept soundly and sweetly, undisturbed by the loud bellowing of the iron-mouthed bullies.

Our party was divided into three watches, who were to fight the battery by turns. We became excellent practitioners in gunnery, knocking off with great accuracy the unfortunate bullocks as they were turned out to graze on the ramparts; our aim would not have disgraced that of riflemen. Lieutenant B—gl—d outdid his competitors in these trials of skill ; the shot directed by him was certain of reaching its mark : perhaps the best encomium bestowed upon his dexterity, was the frequent request of the artillery officer, to take the exact elevation of the gun previously to its being discharged. Jack christened the twenty-four pounder used with such admirable effect, "Bl—dy murder:" not the most agreeably sounding appellation, but tolerably expressive of his opinion.

On the third day from the commencement of the bombardment, the enemy was observed from our position preparing to make a sally upon the works on the opposite side to ourselves. Our guns were all loaded with shrapnel shells under the guidance of the artillery officer attached to the battery. The French had formed, and their leading files had commenced marching off, when the first shrapnel burst slap in among them, and left a fearful gap; others followed in quick succession, apparently with the like effect, for the party immediately broke and retreated out of the line of our fire. The same afternoon we gave them a second edition of the first day's discharge, which was but feebly returned. Edevain, the gunner of the Pompée, was this day seriously wounded: the loss of his services was much felt. He was a man far superior to the station he then filled, having regularly served his time and passed for a lieutenant. On our return to England, through the representation of the Commodore, he was rewarded with the commission he had so long yearned for, but of which he had abandoned all hope.

I wish that all commanding officers were fully alive to the interest they might inspire, and to the grateful feelings they would inevitably secure to themselves, did they more carefully appreciate the abilities and investigate the exertions of modest men of worth and talent—men who, destitute of interest and powerful connexions, continue to perform their duties zealously, fight gallantly, struggle nobly, and frequently die in their country's service, unrewarded, neglected, and forgotten. These are the subjects that merit the peculiar attention and good offices of commanding officers; they have it in their power to represent the several claims of deserving men in the proper quarter, and, if they fail in the observance of this positive duty, they have much to answer for. By such flagrant injustice, genius is not only crippled, a sensitive mind cruelly wounded, and meritorious exertions paralyzed, but the injury done is two-fold,—the individual and the public are alike sufferers, the latter losing the benefit of the promising talents of a zealous and well-disposed servant. The loss, taken in the aggregate, may be considered trifling, yet it often amounts to more than all the good which a commanding officer does to the community at large.

The power of obtaining rewards and benefits, or of being in any way instrumental to the happiness of our fellow-creatures, is productive of pure unsullied pleasure to the nobly constituted mind; but if this enviable power is the privileged attribute of a commanding officer, and he is free to unite the yearnings of a generous heart to the prescribed duties of his station, it is not mere invective to assert, that shame rests with the man who from paltry motives, indifference, or other causes, remains callous to the zealous services of persons who naturally and confidently regard him as the channel through which their respective merits should be acknowledged and represented. To cultivate a grateful temper among those around us, and upon whose exertions we hope to lay the basis of our own fame and reputation, is not only politic, but calls forth better, nobler feelings; and the same principle which is acutely touched with the kindness of a benefactor, is also capable of being deeply affected by far higher considerations, and of becoming, under the powerful influence of that affection, a source of the purest joy and most exalted virtue. It is an attribute of our position, when impartially used, that is to be cherished above all others we may possess.

On the morning of the 22nd of February, the white flag was flying on the fortress, and the fire ceased, only to be speedily renewed, the object of the enemy being merely to gain time. Our grand mortar-battery was chiefly directed against their principal magazine, and so effectually had it done its work, that the enemy, fearful of the dreadful consequences of an explosion, had hoisted a truce, in the hope of being enabled to remove their powder to a securer situation; this, however, had been foreseen and the Frenchmen were disappointed in their object. I had arrived with my party in the battery the moment the order was given to recommence hostilities, which was briskly executed. The fire of the enemy became extremely animated; they were quite refreshed from the short cessation we had allowed them. My four hours' duty had nearly expired, in five minutes more I should have been relieved, when I was placed *hors de combat* for a short time, and was carried off to the surgeon in the rear. The real injury bore no proportion to the extent of mischief which my appearance presented. I had just been laid on the grass, when my messmate who was to relieve me, passed by; I heard him inquire, "Who is it?" for I suppose I was not recognizable. "Mr. S." was the reply.

"Poor Jemmy!" and he turned to pursue his way to the battery, expressing his regret for his lost friend.

"He is only wounded," added the surgeon; and in an instant my messmate was joined by another, and they were both kneeling at my side. The affectionate and joyous interest they expressed at finding I had not been knocked off, soothed the excruciating pain I began to experience, after recovering the use of my senses. There is something magical in kind words and anxious solicitude; and though I could not reply to their friendly inquiries, a warm pressure of the hand convinced them I was not so bad as appearances indicated; and they proceeded to take their share of the Frenchman's ire. My own party being relieved, I was removed by them to the encampment, where the Commodore soon visited me, and immediately ordered the surgeon to send me on board. Fancying, however, I was not so bad as to require removal, I persuaded the medical man to allow me to remain where I was; for which the poor fellow got a rap on the knuckles, and I was despatched by the first boat that quitted the shore.

On reaching the ship, the first lieutenant, whose kindness and friendship towards me had been far greater than I merited, was looking over the side, and hailed me :

"Well, Master Jemmy, have you had enough of the shore this time? Why, what have the Frenchmen been doing to make you look so black upon the matter? Come, we must try and set you to rights again;" and I was once more installed in his cabin. Bones remained as first lieutenant of the Pompée, after the Commodore quitted her, and was in the action she sustained with the Hautpoult, for which he was promoted to the rank of Commander. Poor fellow! he retained his sense just long enough to know that his services had at last been acknowledged, and died a few hours afterwards on board the Pompée.

The gallant exertions of our brethren the red-coats, with whom the blue-jackets cordially united, were soon crowned with success, by the surrender of Fort Bourbon, or Dessaix, and the consequent submission of the whole island. Commodore Cockburn was appointed one of the commissioners on the part of the British, in the treaty for the surrender. The garrison (upwards of three thousand) were allowed to march out with the honours of war, and were to be conveyed to France in English transports, and there landed, provided an equal number of Englishmen were exchanged for them.

I was soon enabled to visit the fort. Never was a scene of greater devastation presented; every building was knocked down, and the earth literally ploughed up by our shells. The principal magazine, to which the mortars were directed, was so injured that it was expected every moment the shells would penetrate it, and cause it to explode. Their guns were upset, the platforms destroyed, and the destruction caused by our ricochet shot was murderous; our batteries were so judiciously placed, that the one opposed by the French to the sailors' guns was enfiladed by our's to the left, whilst our fire again was equally destructive to that in face of the other. I observed that two guns had been blown up, and buried beneath the level of the platform, by our thirteen-inch shells having fallen obliquely under them. The bomb-proofs were untenable: the dreadful state of filth and corruption in the casemates, &c. is too disgusting and horrible to describe; the air was positively infected with the noxious effluvia emitted from the slaughtered bodies of the garrison, the carcases of animals, and the mass of abomination that infested the whole place.

It was the first time I had witnessed the effects of a bombardment; it is one I shall never forget, and I left the scene of desolation and murderous havoc fully impressed with the extent of horrors entailed by a state of warfare. No alternative but surrender was left to the gallant governor— no shelter was afforded to his men from our unerring fire;* added to which, disease, with all its

* Upwards of 25,000 shells were thrown into Fort Bourbon during this short bombardment.

frightful concomitants, arising from their deplorable situation in a tropical climate, had broken out, and in a few days must have carried off the majority. To have inhabited the fort would have been attended with imminent risk, till a regular purification had been effected.

It is singular that the French complained of having suffered severely by the ricochetting shots from Fort Royal, a spot which they had absolutely considered as insignificant, and as affording no ground for annoyance by shot. The elevation of our guns, from the battery formed within its walls, (if my memory is correct,) could not have been less than thirty degrees; the after-trucks were taken off, and those before raised, to attain the necessary elevation. The charge was regulated merely to pitch the shot over the walls, and away it bounded like a cricket-ball the whole range of the fort. Notwithstanding all these circumstances, Villaret Joyeuse was tried and disgraced for giving up the fort, and shortly after his return to France died of a broken heart on his own estate in Normandy.

Arrangements were immediately entered into

to embark the captive garrison. The Commodore was to take charge of them to Europe, for which purpose he shifted his broad pendant to the Belleisle, into which ship I accompanied him; and in less than three weeks we were prepared to sail, in company with the Argo, forty-four, and the transports with the French prisoners.

During the time of preparation, I paid a visit to St. Pierre, certainly one of the prettiest towns in the West Indies. The French flag was still kept flying there, for the purpose of deceiving the enemy's vessels: several came in, and were not aware of the fall of the island until the English officers went on board to take possession of them.

Before our departure, a Court-martial was held on board the Pompée on the officers and men of his Majesty's late brig the Carnation, which had been captured by a French sloop of war, under circumstances extremely galling to the pride of the British navy. It was an event which excited great interest. The Carnation was one of the finest of our eighteen-gun brigs, but she was manned by a worthless crew. A fatality appeared to hang over her when she fell in with the French brig; for the first broadside killed her Commander, Captain Charles Mars Gregory, and shortly afterwards the first and second lieutenants were severely wounded: the latter, James Fitzmaurice, in a gallant attempt to lead on the Carnation's men to board the enemy. The Master was mortally wounded; and the command of the vessel devolved upon the boatswain, who, observing the Frenchman waver, called on the men to board the enemy's vessel. At this critical moment the sergeant of marines turned recreant and fled below, and was followed in his dastardly retreat by the majority of the survivors. The French Captain was also killed, and his crew had in like manner started from their guns. Thus were the two vessels lying alongside of each other, with only a few brave spirits remaining on either deck, when the enemy's second in command, astonished at the cessation of his adversary's fire, peeped over the bulwarks, and, discovering the desertion of her decks, succeeded in rallying his people, and boarded on the forecastle of the Carnation, which was gallantly but ineffectually contested by the boatswain and two or three of his men. In a few minutes she became a prize to the Frenchman, and was safely conducted into Cul-de-sac Marin at Martinique, where she was destroyed on our making good our landing. The surviving officers and crew had been received in exchange on board the Pompée before the arrival of the expedition, and among them was the sergeant of marines.

The Court-martial would have been summoned immediately, but for the operations commenced for the reduction of the island. As soon as this event took place, the order for its assembling was given. By some oversight, or, which is more likely, a desire on the part of the first lieutenant of the Pompée to give the unhappy sergeant a chance of averting the destiny that hung over him, he sent him on shore as one of the party to work at the batteries. Had the sergeant taken advantage of this opportunity, he would probably have escaped the ignominious death that ended his career; but here again he turned tail, and was remanded on board as a prisoner.

The court rigidly examined into every particular, and, after a patient investigation of all the facts, honourably acquitted the officers, it being proved that the nature of their wounds was such as to preclude the possibility of their taking any further part in the action; but the unhappy sergeant was condemned to be hung, and thirty-two of his cowardly followers to run him up to the yard-arm, and to be afterwards transported for fourteen years to Botany Bay.

From the conclusive evidence that was produced, the fate of the poor wretch was manifest. The stillness of the tomb reigned throughout the court as the Judge Advocate read the sentence. The start of horror which seized the doomed man as his death-knell rang on his ear, was succeeded by a calm resigned deportment which astonished the audience; and as he left the court he respectfully bowed to his judges, without one pleading look for mercy.

There is something so fearfully awful, so indescribably overwhelming in the condemnation of a fellow-creature to death, that, however deeply he may have sinned against a particular code of laws enacted for the well-being of the country, and though he may be pronounced deserving of the fate that consigns him to the hands of the executioner, yet we tremble, and an involuntary thrill of horror creeps through our frames, as we intently fix our eyes upon the living breathing form before us sentenced to die by the decree of his fellow men,—to perish in the vigour of manhood,—to expiate with the breath of life (God's own and precious gift,) an offence originating too often, it is to be feared, in some physical derangement of constitution, or proceeding from that mysterious influence which at times attacks and prostrates the energies of man,—mocking his free agency, and proclaiming his degeneracy.

Whence springs the wild anomalous feeling that prompts us to look with enthusiastic ardour on the slaughter of the battle-field? to deal and receive the blow that may dissolve the mystic union of the incorruptible soul with the corruptible body? our bosoms heaving with swelling pride, strangers to remorseful pangs or pity's throb. Await awhile! the battle is over, and a solitary being is doomed to die:—women's softness steals over our senses, an indefinable rush of harrowing sensations crowd upon us, reminding us that we are men—inheritors of frail erring mortality!

The sentence was confirmed by the Commander-in-chief, and in a few fleeting hours the execution was to take place on board the ship of the second in command. The fatal morning was ushered in by the melancholy and necessary preparations: they were witnessed by our crew with settled gloom: the temporary stage erected over the cat-head was ready, the rope rove at the fore yard-arm was stopped into the bunt of the yard. The signal gun was fired from the Admiral's ship for the boats of the fleet to attend punishment, and repeated by the Pompée. The unhappy man was engaged with the chaplain in deep prayer, as the report of the gun struck upon his ear: it passed unheeded, so intently, so fervently were his thoughts fixed upon eternity—

> "That undiscover'd bourne,
> From whence no traveller returns."

From the period of his condemnation his conduct was edifying and devout: he expected no mercy,—he sued for none. To have judged him by his behaviour after sentence, it would have been difficult to believe that he could have ever failed in courage or fortitude. The boats assembled around, marines were stationed in the bows and stern-sheets, the hands were turned up, the rigging of the different ships of the squadron filled with their respective crews dressed in their best and uncovered. All was ready, and the sergeant walked from the cabin on to the quarter-deck, attended by the clergyman. An awful stillness pervaded the ship; the sentence of the court, and the order for the execution, were read. His demeanour was so correct, so firm, and yet so submissively resigned, that the feelings of the bystanders were strongly, painfully excited in his favour: the fault for which he was about to suffer was forgotten in the admiration of the Christian fortitude with which he encountered his fate. Before his arms were pinioned, he requested to address the ship's company: he spoke to them in an impressive and collected manner; he acknowledged the justice of his sentence; called upon all those who were about to witness his ignominious death to remember they owed their lives to the service of their country;—that by having yielded to unmanly fears he had led others astray, and that he felt he had fairly forfeited his life to the offended laws of his country; adding, that he hoped his fate would be considered a sufficient atonement for his offence. The address was delivered in a tone of deep humility, and he concluded by returning thanks for the kindness he had received. The silent tears might be seen coursing each other down the furrowed and bronzed cheek of many a hardy veteran. The scene became overpoweringly distressing as the signal was given to move forward to the scaffold. As he passed the main rigging, a suppressed groan, and " God bless you!" might be plainly heard to issue from the overcharged hearts of the crew. On the gangway the clergyman, taking the lead, commenced in a deep sonorous voice the service for the dead over a warm, animated body—

" In the midst of life we are in death."

I have often heard that beautiful prayer, as the cold inanimate forms of my shipmates and friends have been plunged into the deep, but never did it make so forcible an impression upon me as on that morning; my tears were not to be repressed. Arrived on the forecastle, he again thanked the clergyman, and with a resolute step mounted the scaffold. He continued absorbed in prayer until the cap was drawn over his eyes. In a few seconds he dropped the handkerchief; the gun exploded under his feet, and in the smoke of the discharge his luckless and condemned shipmates ran him up to the yard-arm. Death must have been instantaneous, for the body never moved. It was an awful, heart-rending ceremony, such as might shake a man with iron nerves.

It is a humiliating and degrading spectacle to see a human being hung up like a dog, and I cannot reconcile my mind to the infliction of death by this means in the navy. As respects the deliberate murderer, or the hardened felon of a hundred crimes, such a revolting end may perhaps add to the ignominy of the decree; but to pursue the same method in an honourable profession of arms, whose members may perchance forget their duty and incur the penalty of death, renders bitterness doubly bitter to the unfortunate man, engenders a feeling of deep degradation among his officers and shipmates, and uselessly sullies the high character of excellence for which our naval regulations should stand unrivalled.

The offences for which sailors may be supposed to deserve death, while in active service and under martial law, are frequently such as under other circumstances could scarcely expose them to severe public correction. If, then, they render themselves, or are rendered by the necessities of the country, amenable to severe laws, it is not too much to expect that, when visited with punishment, sailors should die like men, and not be hanged like dogs.

CHAPTER VII.

Quit the Pompée.—Reception of the late Governor and suite on board the Belleisle.—Bills of Exchange for Prize-money.—Departure from Port Royal.—Devotion of his Officers to Napoleon.—Arrival in Quiberon Bay.—Negotiation for Exchange of Prisoners.—A Frenchman's Trick.—Departure of the French Governor and suite.—My anxiety to proceed to London.—An unlucky meeting.—A Rebuke.—Lucky Escape.—The expedition to Walcheren.—Disembarkation of the Troops.—Investment of Flushing.—Gallantry of the Raven brig.—Force the passage between Cadsand and Flushing.—Completion of the Batteries against Flushing —The Bombardment.—Surrender of the Town.—A French Sergeant's remark.—Horrors of War.—Freedom of England from its Devastation.—Claims of our Defenders on the National Gratitude.

We quitted the Pompée with feelings of regret: her superior good qualities and sailing placed her far above the rest of the squadron; but she was too efficient a vessel, and too lately from England, to be sent home; while the Belleisle, requiring a complete repair, remained on the station. Lieutenants M–l–d and B–gl–d accompanied the Commodore into his new ship. The former became our first lieutenant; he had attended our chief during the whole of his arduous and laborious operations on shore, and received his commission on our arrival in England: he had been our second lieutenant in the Phaeton, and was universally esteemed for his kindness of heart, decision, coolness in danger, and perfect knowledge of his profession: he was one of those who cannot be forgotten.

The garrison embarked, and the late governor and suite were received on board the Belleisle with the honorary marks of distinction due to a brave enemy, and with the feeling of respect his conduct to our countrymen (whom the fortune of war had placed in his power) richly merited. It must have mitigated his unpleasant feelings to find himself placed with the man for whom he had already felt the strongest sentiments of respect. Admiral Villaret Joyeuse was esteemed a generous enemy, and this feeling was fully displayed by the successful party, who wished to introduce an article in the treaty stipulating for the free return of himself and suite to France; but the gallant old gentleman declined this mark of favour, preferring to share the fate of the garrison. Admiral Villaret Joyeuse commanded the French fleet in the memorable action with Earl Howe on the first of June 1794. A number of military and naval French officers embarked on board the Belleisle, so that we were completely full; their natural *gaïeté de cœur* enlivened the passage.

Before we set sail, Mr. Maxwell, the Agent who had followed the expedition to Martinique, gave us bills upon England for the amount of prize-money (a considerable sum) due to those officers and men of the Pompée who had accompanied the Commodore into the Belleisle. The bills were protested, and sent back to the West Indies; and the first news we heard in return was, that Mr. Maxwell had departed this life, and had died insolvent. This was my second stroke of ill fortune: I had now lost all that I had gained both in the East and West Indies.

We took our departure from Port Royal, in the middle of March accompanied by the **Argo**, forty-four, and the transports filled with French troops. We ran down the islands, passed close to St. Christopher's, whence we were saluted, and clearing the Sombrero Channel, entered upon the open sea.

The time passed agreeably enough; we were on the best possible terms with our French companions, many of whom were in our berth. The laugh, the song, and joke went merrily round; and while we laughed at their attempts to converse in English, they returned the compliment in the best-humoured manner by smiling at the blunders made in their own language.

The deep devotion of the majority of the officers to Napoleon was strikingly conspicuous, and, though all hope of being restored to their country was destroyed by the refusal of their ruler to exchange them, and their bitter disappointment had for the moment drawn down upon him denunciations deep and heavy, in thus casting from him men who had served and fought faithfully under his banners, all thoughts of self, and the hardships of a long imprisonment in an enemy's country, vanished into air, when the last vessel that took the Governor on shore arrived, bringing with it the news of Napoleon's glittering success at Echmuhl: one spontaneous burst of devoted enthusiastic feeling evinced how completely he had regained his wonted empire over their minds. A *capitaine de frégate*, who had been personally noticed by Napoleon, and brought forward by him in consequence of having distinguished himself under his searching eye, was one of our passengers: he regarded that extraordinary man as a superior being, as one whose name ought never to be lightly mentioned; he appeared to adore his chief. Whenever he pronounced or heard the word l'Empereur, his hand was mechanically lifted to his hat, and his head uncovered. This act of respect being remarked by some of our gay mischievous officers, *Monsieur le capitaine de frégate* was frequently engaged in conversation for the purpose of seeing how often in a certain space of time his devotion would lead him to uncover at the mention of his sovereign's name. The joke was repeated too often, and the merriment of the bystanders discovered to the astonished and deeply wounded Frenchman. The folly of the trial was thoroughly felt, and a proportionate degree of sorrow at having, by the indulgence of an unwarrantable freak, harassed the feelings of a brave, devoted, and worthy seaman. His concluding remark, " *Je suis prisonnier, mais vous n'avez pas le droit de m'insulter,*" conveyed a merited reproach to the instigators and performers of this thoughtless fancy. All the apologies, all the advances that were made to promote a reconciliation, were of no avail; he could not forget it, and he rigidly avoided all future friendly intercourse with the officers.

At the end of April we arrived safely with our charge in Quiberon Bay, when a flag-of-truce was immediately despatched to the shore. A favourable answer was received, accompanied by a request that we would move higher up the bay, to afford greater facility of communication. The Belleisle therefore moved up, but the Argo, with the transports, were anchored off Hedic Island. The negotiation for the exchange appeared to be going on swimmingly; the French commissioner went so far as to request the names of any of our friends who might be prisoners in France, and that they should be returned among the number exchanged. With what feelings of delight I inscribed the names of my former messmates and officers in the Blanche, and what pleasurable emotions filled my mind at the opportunity of becoming, as I hoped, an humble instrument in effecting their deliverance! The visits of the Frenchman increased this flattering belief: orders had been given for the march of the requisite number of English prisoners, and on such a day they would arrive. Thus were we deceived, when in point of fact not a single individual was *en route* for that purpose.

When the day arrived previous to that on which our poor countrymen were expected, the cunning Frenchman, under the idea that he had completely hoodwinked the Commodore by the plausible manner in which he conducted himself, made his appearance on board with all the confidence of success. He communicated the pleasng intelligence that the English prisoners were within a few miles of the coast; that same evenng would witness the arrival of the advanced division at Vannes, and the next day the whole body would have arrived. To accommodate the Commodore, and that he might be prepared to receive them, he had ordered off a sufficient number of small vessels to land the Frenchmen;—and in fact a musquito fleet was making its appearance for that purpose. Cleverly as the crafty Frenchman carried on the farce of candour, he had not blinded our chief, who at once completely upset the wily schemes of the emissary, by stating that he was delighted at the prospect of the speedy termination of the object of his visit by the arrival of his countrymen, but that he must decline permitting his prisoners to land till the following day, when, for every boat-load of Englishmen brought off, an equal number of Frenchmen should be despatched in exchange.

The politic envoy made much ado about the honour of the Great Nation, and having vainly endeavoured to combat the determination of the Commodore, retired in pretended displeasure at the insult offered in doubting his word. The foiled negociator and his small fry of craft retook their way to the harbour. The next day a communication from the baffled Frenchman made known that the truce was ended, and that no further intercourse with the shore would be allowed, nor would any exchange take place : thus endeavouring to hide, under the cloak of offended dignity, an unworthy and dishonourable deceit. There is the strongest reason to believe that not an Englishman was in the neighbourhood,—that none had even started from the prisons.

We immediately rejoined the convoy, and preparations were made for our departure. An aid-de-camp of Villaret Joyeuse was without delay forwarded to L'Orient, to state to the authorities, that, on their despatching a vessel, the late governor and his suite would be permitted to land : the return of the messenger in the expected vessel was the signal for taking leave of their attentive host. They evidently felt sincere regret at parting with one whose courtesy and kindness had obliterated from their minds his character as an enemy to their country. The niece of the governor, an amiable, interesting girl, was much affected, and on being placed in the barge burst into tears. As the boat lay on her oars to receive the salute that was paid to his excellency, she never lifted up her head, and appeared buried in grief; the waving of her handkerchief, as she stepped on the deck of the vessel that was to convey her to friends and home, appeared to renew her regrets, and she instantly descended to the cabin.

Having fulfilled the articles of the capitulation as far as came within the power of the Commodore, we left the French coast, and proceeded to Spithead, whence the unfortunate prisoners were conveyed to Porchester Castle.

My anxiety to proceed to London had so far got the better of my discretion, that before we came to an anchor I preferred a request to that end: the result was such as my sober senses should have taught me. The Commodore landed, and no sooner was he clear of the ship than I applied to the Captain with so much earnestness that I succeeded in my suit, upon an understanding that my leave was granted only for the purpose of visiting the shore, and that, if by any chance I met the Commodore in London, the permission was to rest upon that plea. Muffled up in my great coat I mounted the roof of the mail, while my Commodore was snugly ensconced inside; and so far escaped detection. My unlucky star was, however, in the ascendant.

On the day of my arrival, as I was carelessly enjoying a lounge along the Strand, I was suddenly brought up by running slap on board the Commodore as he was crossing the pavement from Coutts's to step into his carriage. The shock was sufficient to deaden his way, and fixing his eyes upon the cause of it, " You sir, when did you come to town?"—" This morning, sir."— " Indeed! you have made wonderful haste; now try if you can get on board again equally quick. I have a letter for the first lieutenant; come to my lodgings for it at four o'clock: in the mean time go and secure your place by the coach, and remember my letter is to be delivered on board before noon to-morrow." I stammered and stuttered, and doubtless looked tolerably foolish: unable to make any good excuse, I shuffled off to the coach-office, musing in no very pleasant humour upon the mutability and destruction of a giddy-pated reefer's engagements. No loop-hole was left for me to creep out at; I was fairly caught. The letter and my unlucky self were safe on board the Belleisle at the appointed time.

My scheme for pleasure in London having been thus unceremoniously knocked on the head, a few days saw me on another expedition to the westward. I suppose I considered myself as entitled to some indemnity, or fancied the Commodore's absence was a guarantee for my safety, for I outstayed my leave so long that I returned only in the nick of time to prevent the ominous R being affixed to my name by the clerk of the cheque. I found that Captain C— had hoisted his pendant on board the Belleisle as a private ship, but that he had not yet returned from London. Our excellent first lieutenant had been promoted; Lieut. W., our second, had succeeded him in that responsible office; and the ship was fitting to join the grand expedition then on the *tapis*. Orders had been received to curtail my powers of locomotion, and I was kept close as wax to the ship. I received from my Captain, on his return, an unenviable lecture upon my misdeeds, and I am bound to confess I richly deserved it.

Our noble first, with whom I was always upon the best terms, at length took compassion upon my pitiable condition, and allowed me to accompany him one evening on shore, where, doffing my uniform, and clothing myself in shore-going togs, I regarded myself as secure from prying observation. It was the period of Free-mart fair, and Saunders with all his equestrian troop formed one of the great points of attraction. I entered the booth, and, taking my station in one of the side galleries immediately over the horses, my attention became riveted upon the performance, so that I neither observed the company assembling to the right or left. But the sounds of a well-known voice directly behind me, upset all my complacency, and made my blood tingle again; they proceeded from Captain C— and Lord A. B—k. I dared not turn my head the eighth of an inch; the corner of the well-known gold-laced hat protruded over my head; it kept nodding forward with provoking pertinacity; there seemed to be an irresistible attraction between it and my pericranium; detection appeared certain; all retreat was cut off. Hemmed in on all sides, I was in a perfect quandary, when a happy idea suggested itself to my worried mind. The loose unnailed and open planks, upon which I was standing, prompted me to play one of harlequin's tricks, and take my departure between them. Having found with my feet a sufficient space for a prosperous exit, I rested my hands on the bar in front, and then passing my feet clear of impediments through the aperture, I quitted my hold, and down I slipped upon the horses underneath. It was supposed to be an accident, and as I had no wish to enlighten the kind souls above upon the subject, I took care not to look up, but quickly made my escape under the horses' bellies. A fatality attended me whenever I broke through the Captain's orders; by some means I invariably betrayed myself. This adventure so alarmed and convinced me there was no struggling with unhappy conjunctions and malign influences, that I wrote to Captain C— the next day, requesting to be allowed to see him, when I made suitable excuses, and it being stated by Lieutenant W. that I had received conditional leave of absence from Captain B. my transgressions were pardoned, and I was again reinstated in his favour.

All was now bustle in getting ready for sea: the lower deck was prepared for the reception of troops, and the guns landed; the upper tier of casks got out of the hold, and stables fitted up for horses: in short, we were turned, with many others, into a regular trooper. Spithead was crowded with men-of-war destined for the same service. Portsmouth was filled with officers of both services, and their friends; every house of accommodation was overflowing: it was a glorious harvest for the tradesmen.

By the middle of July all was ready, and shortly afterwards the troops were marched down to Southsea beach, and embarked in beautiful order. Two thirds of that crack regiment of Highlanders, the 71st, commanded by the late Sir Dennis Pack, fell to our share.

Under the orders of Rear-admiral Otway, the Portsmouth division, consisting of a strong squadron of line-of-battle ships, temporarily fitted up as ourselves, and filled with our brethren in arms, each in charge of a gun-boat, took its departure from Spithead. On our arrival in the Downs, which was crowded with shipping, the division of the fleet under Lord Gardner, proceeded to the Dutch coast. We followed the succeeding day.

It is a rare sight to see such a congregation of vessels as were then assembled. As far as the eye could reach from the mast-head, the sea appeared alive with shipping, from the stately seventy-four, the gallant frigates, and the dashing sloops, down to the innumerable fry of gun-brigs, cutters, gun-boats, and transports, which thickly dotted the bosom of the German Ocean. Never was a more gallant array sent forth from the shores of Albion, and never perhaps were her sons doomed to be more bitterly disappointed than with the result of this expedition.

A stiff breeze brought us speedily in sight of the enemy's coast; in the evening we anchored off Walcheren. The weather precluded all hope of landing that evening. At daylight the signal was made to weigh and follow the Admiral, who stood towards the Roompot; we steered after him, when the North Sea pilots, thunderstruck at the bold attempt, gave up charge of the ship, declaring to the captain that he would inevitably run her aground: he was too intently engaged to heed them, farther than to announce his determination to take charge of the ship himself, and they might go anywhere, so that they would get out of his way. The leading ships showed the soundings, from eight to nine fathoms; as they entered the channel they decreased to six — five and a half— five—four and a half: the water became perfectly smooth, and we all reached the snug anchorage of the Roompot in safety, (three or four excepted,) abreast a beach on which scarce a ripple broke.

Preparations were immediately commenced for disembarking the troops; all the flat-bottomed and ships' boats were hoisted out; the gun-boats brought alongside for their guns, and the launches armed. The troops were soon in the boats, but, the tide running very strong, it was found impracticable to push off till it slackened; they therefore remained alongside and astern of their respective ships, with their divisional pendants flying. It was a gallant sight. The enemy was seen along and behind the dikes, but there appeared no disposition on his part to come upon the plain of sand between the water's edge and the embankment. When the rapidity of the tide subsided, the signal "Prepare to land" was hoisted, and the boats, under the command and direction of Lord Amelius Beauclerk and Captain Cockburn, were assembled in beautiful order according to their several divisions; while the bombs and small craft got under weigh, and, taking their stations inshore to cover the disembarkation, scoured the beach. At the appointed signal, led on by Captain C——, they all pushed for the beach in line. The troops landed, immediately formed, and marched forward to meet the enemy, who offered but a slight resistance to them from behind the dikes. As soon as our fellows crowned the bank, a hot fire of musketry announced the work of contention. In the mean time, the boats returned for a second cargo;—on reaching the beach with our gallant freight, a number of French prisoners were ready for embarkation.

The force opposed to the landing was trifling, and, finding resistance useless, they retreated to Terveer, closely followed by the intrepid Colonel Pack and his Highlanders, who had nearly succeeded in entering the gates with the rear of the enemy; but our soldiers suffered severely from the heavy fire of grape that assailed them on their retreat. During the day all the troops intended to be landed were thrown on shore, and they took up a position towards Middleburg, a great part of the enemy's forces being in front of them. The following day all the gun-boats and bombs proceeded against Terveer, which was immediately bombarded. No boats could have been better adapted to the service, for which they were especially built; each carried a long twenty-four pounder forward, and a carronade of the same calibre abaft. They swam so low upon the water, and presented so small a body to fire at, that there was great difficulty in striking them. In three days, with the assistance of the bombs, they obliged the town to surrender;—our loss amounted to three gun-boats, and several men killed and wounded. The army having previously advanced and taken possession of Middleburg, drove the enemy into Flushing, and commenced the investment of that place.

It was determined to move up all the small craft and lesser frigates into the Scheldt by the passage of the Sloe, round Terveer and the Ramakins. The latter fort having been abandoned, the passage was clear, until we arrived at its entrance into the Scheldt. The difficulty was great in passing through so narrow a channel without pilots, and considerably augmented by the rapidity of the tides. Vessels were aground in every direction. Indomitable perseverance on the part of Captain C— (who had the conducting of this service,) and the commanding officers under him, conquered the intricacies and difficulties that presented themselves every ten minutes to the view and patience of the different commanders.

After leaving the Ramakins, all the vessels were obliged to pass close to a two-gun battery which the enemy had erected on the dike beyond the outworks of Flushing. The mischief these guns did us was wicked. Two twenty-four pounders were landed at the Ramakins. During the same night our engineers had thrown up a battery on the same dike, within four hundred yards of the enemy's, and at daybreak the Frenchmen's attention was in some measure diverted from the blue-jackets on the water, to their disagreeable neighbours our brother blues in the newly-constructed battery. The following night another battery was erected within two hundred yards of the enemy, and the guns were conveyed into it before morning. The fire of the artillery-men was beautiful; Johnny was scarcely allowed an opportunity to load his pieces, and our fellows had already given them the trouble of bringing up fresh guns in lieu of those they had dismounted. It was amusing to see the Frenchmen bobbing about whenever they expected to be saluted. The ships were no longer so much annoyed by their great guns, but they brought down field pieces, and placed them in a sheltered position, which inflicted some severe loss upon us. Lieut. Bigland carrying orders in Captain C—'s gig had a round-shot sent through her, fortunately without hurting any one.

As this position commanded the entrance to the passage round by the Ramakins, and had seriously mauled us, it was determined to storm it. This duty was confided to our late shipmates the 71st, and was gallantly executed by Colonel Pack with a detachment of his regiment: the loss was severe, but might be considered as trivial in comparison with the service effected. It was carried at about three or four in the morning. I entered the work at day-light: friend and foe lay mingled together in one confused mass, and the worst picture of war was presented to our view; the English bayonet had done its work on the bodies of the gallant Frenchmen. One of the officers of the 71st, a fine young man, full of hope and high in spirits at the prospect of gleaning some ears of the harvest of glory that was opening to his view, lay extended on a bed of clotted gore, covered with wounds. He had dashingly pushed on in advance, and had speedily met the death of a British soldier, showing a brilliant example to the spirited Highlanders who followed him, and who amply avenged the fall of their brave young officer.

Previously to all the gun-boats, bombs, sloops of war, and some of the smaller frigates with a number of transports, entering the Scheldt by the Sloe,—Commodore Sir Edward Owen, lying in the Stein Diep, observed several small schuyts filled with troops attempting to cross over from Cadsand to reinforce the garrison at Flushing. He immediately directed the Raven sixteen-gun brig, Captain Hanchett, to weigh and endeavour to prevent them from reaching their destination. This was effectually performed in a style of gallantry seldom surpassed, to the great delight and admiration of a large body of both army and navy, who were spectators of the action that very soon commenced between the Raven and the batteries on Cadsand and the whole sea-front of Flushing. The expenditure of the enemy in red-hot shot, grape, and shells, upon the little brig, was sufficient to have destroyed fifty such vessels. She was handled and fought in a manner that reflected the greatest credit and honour on her commander, and every individual on board. Latterly she became unmanageable from the wind failing, and having her topmast knocked over the side, her lower masts and all her spars badly wounded, sails and rigging cut to pieces. The ebb-tide drifted her out of gun-shot on a sand-bank, from which she was not extricated till the following morning. This brilliant affair on the part of the Raven elicited universal applause from both services. The Commander-in-chief deeming a stronger force requisite, a squadron of frigates was selected to force the passage between Cadsand and Flushing. When the wind became favourable, the Lavinia, Lord W. Stuart, with nine others stood in; they were saluted by a heavy fire from both shores, which was as smartly returned. The passage was accomplished with trifling loss. It was a beautiful sight as seen from the dike near the Ramakins, where Sir Richard Strachan with Captain C— and several officers had stationed themselves to behold the result. When the ships had anchored, I took the Commander-in-chief off in the captain's gig to the Lavinia, where he hoisted his flag *pro tempore*. A thirteen-inch shell fell on board one of our frigates, L'Aigle, and passing through her decks and the scuttle of her bread-room, exploded, killing one man, and wounding four others, shivering to atoms all the bulk-heads in the gun-room: the steward, in the after gun-room, miraculously escaped unhurt; had it fallen one foot farther forward, it must have penetrated the after-magazine, and blown the ship up.

Two days after this dashing entrée (August 13th,) the different batteries against Flushing were completed. The flotilla of gun-boats, bombs, &c. under the command of Commodore C—, who had again hoisted his broad pendant on board the Plover, were constantly engaging the sea-front of the enemy's defences during the day, and were kept under weigh on the weather-tide during the night, between Cadsand and Flushing, to prevent any further supplies or reinforcements being thrown into the latter place: upwards of three thousand men had crossed over before we got a sufficient number of small craft in the river to prevent them.

The gun-boats, which were generally stationed out of range of grape from the walls, were as galling to the enemy as a nest of hornets would have been about their ears. It appears wonderful, considering the number of hours the boats were daily under fire during the siege, that the loss on our side should have been so trifling as it really was.

The opening out of the batteries was a splendid sight. The first flight of Congreve's rockets failed in the expectation formed of them, the distance being too great; but they soon attained the proper range: the terrific roaring of these destructive weapons, with their fiery trains, produced a magnificent effect at night. The fires that blazed in different parts of the beleaguered town, too plainly showed the efficacy of the different projectiles that were showered upon the devoted city. I remember counting eighteen shells at one time in the air.

Sir Richard Strachan had determined upon bringing the squadron of line-of-battle ships into the Scheldt on the opening out of the land batteries, but was unable to effect it till the following day. The sight of the frigates gallantly forcing the passage, which had been deemed impracticable by the enemy for line-of-battle ships, was a proud and gratifying spectacle; but the approach of the line-of-battle ships, led on by the Commander-in-chief, was most imposing. The fire of the flotilla and bombs redoubled, nor were our batteries on shore less vigorous as our ships entered the channel; but, tremendous as it was, their roar was lost in the stunning broadsides that were opened upon the sea-batteries as the squadron passed on. All the ships succeeded in the attempt, except the Admiral's ship, the St. Domingo, and Rear-Admiral Lord Gardner in the Blake; they grounded abreast the enemy's principal battery. The Commodore quickly proceeded to their assistance. The uninterrupted stream of fire issuing from the vessels' sides, led their anxious friends frequently to fear they were on fire: it was the hottest and most incessant cannonade from ships that I ever witnessed. In a very brief space of time, the whole sea-front opposed to them was silenced, one gun excepted, which being mounted *en barbette* enabled the enemy to continue playing upon them; but as the tide flowed, the ships got off, and took up their anchorage.

I was one of the very few officers who obtained an entrance into the town the first day of the surrender. The principal battery opposed to our ships might not be inaptly compared to a slaughter-house; I remarked one poor devil in a sentry-box with the upper part of his head shot away—a ball had gone through the box, evidently fired from the sailors' battery commanded by Captain Richardson, but it must have been turned from its destructive course by coming in contact with some other object, which gave it the oblique direction that proved fatal to the sentry. The spot appeared completely sheltered from our shot.

I entered into conversation with an old veteran French sergeant, who, being proud of a little smattering of English, conversed in our native tongue. He had been quartered at the gun immediately adjoining the tower which caught fire during the contest. On describing the effect of our fire, which he considered as impossible to stand against, he apologised for the batteries being silenced by the following emphatic speech —" Me fire one gun,—two gun,—*G—damn* English ship fire fifty hondred."

The upper parts of the houses situated at the back of the batteries exposed to our fire were literally knocked to pieces. The devastation presented throughout the town was terrible and appalling. Numbers of the inhabitants perished from taking shelter in the cellars of their houses, and several melancholy instances were discovered of the annihilation of whole families; the shells having penetrated into their retreats, and exploding buried all those in the ruins who had escaped the effects of the splinters.

There is no scene so deeply distressing to a humane and contemplative mind as that which meets our view immediately after the bombardment of a town. The mischief done to the garrison is sufficiently disastrous; but when a frightful majority of the sufferers are non-combatants, women, children, we in vain essay to stifle the harrowing images that haunt our imagination—of streams of blood and tears of anguish—of the despair, agony, and suffering, that by turns assailed the throbbing breasts of the slaughtered victims around us—of mothers mourning over the bleeding bodies of their little ones—fathers cursing their destroyers—terrified children clinging to dying parents—maddened parents refusing to be comforted—the wise and the virtuous, the wicked and the base, the beautiful and the brave, all engulphed in one common mass of ruin, carnage, and desolation—the homes of childhood, manhood, age, consuming,—the rushing onward of the conquerors, flushed with victory, panting for revenge—the cry for mercy—the patriot's lament—the infant's wail! But amidst the cannon's roar, the deafening shouts of triumph, and far above the shriek of mortal agony—

> The liberated soul ascends
> With rapid flight, spurning
> The shackles of destroying man!

Oh, England! fair, beautiful, and beloved country! "land of my sires," my devotion, my affection; thy peaceful bosom hath not been lacerated by these sores; thy towns have not been bombarded, thy dwellings burnt, thy altars destroyed, thy garners pillaged, thy hearths polluted, or thy daughters insulted. Blood hath not streamed at thy thresholds; thy verdant valleys have not resounded to the din of war, or to the groans of the wounded and the dying; thy hills have not re-echoed to the victor's blast, or thy rivers rocked a victor's fleet; thy cheek hath not blushed with shame, or thy bosom heaved with indignant sobs, at the advance of a licentious soldiery.

Englishmen! fair and generous countrywomen! all these evils have your fellow-creatures suffered and endured; regret not, then, that your purse-strings have been opened to avert the destruction of your household gods. Look around you—read

—travel, and learn to value the blessings ye enjoy; and if ye now in the time of peace, feel an awkward pressure, the inevitable consequence of the past, recollect that ye suffered not in the time of war; and that if your luxuries are now abridged, and your pockets invaded, ye have escaped unharmed in person, unscathed in honour—that ye are happy, rich, and free. Senators, lords of splendid domains, squires of high and low degree, ye that revel in affluence, and ye that dwell in pining discontent, forget not the men who periled life, liberty, and limb for you—who struggled, fought, died for you. Begrudge not the pittance allotted to the widows of the slain and the dead, or the necessary expenditure for the support of the survivors; suffer not the sordid harangues of ambitious men to subdue the generous dictates of British hearts; let not your active defenders live in poverty and die in misery. The storm is past, the danger over, but a time may come when brave and indignant men, proclaimed as they now are a burthen to the state, may demur to spill their heart's blood, and bequeath their families to the equivocal justice of an ungrateful country!

CHAPTER VIII.

Treaty for the evacuation of the works of Flushing—Attempt by the Enemy's gun-boats—Our flotilla—The Army moves towards Bathz—An invitation—Unpleasant result—Agreeable surprise—Appointed Lieutenant to the Resolution—Attacked by the malignant fever—Nominated to His Majesty's Ship F—che—Proceed to the Downs—Ordered into harbour—An altercation and Court-martial—Return home—Appointed to the Myrtle—Captain Napier—Arrive at Lisbon—Turned over to the Barfleur—Ward-room mess of that ship—Scenery about Lisbon—Condition of the city—Approach of the Duke of Wellington towards Lisbon—Superstition—Black crosses —Frequency of murder in Lisbon—Arrival of the Myrtle—Captain Cowan.

The town of Flushing was surrendered by General Monet, after as good a defence as circumstances permitted. Our Commodore was one of the commissioners appointed to treat with the French General for the evacuation of the works. This desirable event being accomplished, the ships moved up towards Bathz. A detachment of our army had previously crossed over to Beveland, and had taken all the river defences in the rear. The enemy abandoned the Fort of Bathz, first spiking the guns, which, however, were quickly rendered serviceable again by our artillerymen. An attempt to retake it was made by the enemy's gun-boats before the arrival of the English flotilla, but they were defeated; several of their boats were disabled, one was sunk, and the rest made off as fast as possible within the boom, drawn across the river at Lillo.*

The British flotilla anchored close up towards Lillo, while the line-of-battle ships were moored from the Doel bank round by Bathz. The former were constantly employed in frustrating the attempts of the enemy to erect batteries on the

* It was amusing to read some of the articles in the newspapers during the late Dutch blockade, setting forth the facility of sending a British fleet to Antwerp; a feat we were unable to perform with one of the largest fleets that ever left England, backed by a fine army of forty thousand men. The authors of the said articles never took into account the intricacy of the navigation, the formidable sea-fronts of Flushing, Cadsand, and the numerous duck-and-drake batteries that line the shores of South Beveland, besides the Forts of Bathz, Lillo, and Liefkinshoek.

shore. The marine artillery displayed much accuracy in dropping their shells; and the practice of the gun-boats in throwing Shrapnel shells was so skilfully correct, that the French succeeded only in forming one battery, which was completed and armed in the course of a night: a brisk fire was opened upon us, but the men were speedily driven from their guns, and the work destroyed by the gun-boats. The advantages afforded us by our elevated view from the mast-heads, were great; we commanded a clear survey of the whole of the flat country that surrounded us, and were enabled by these means to defeat the attempts of the enemy at all points.

The great body of our army had moved up towards Bathz: I was sent one morning before daylight by the Commodore to that place, with a party of carpenters and seamen, to construct a temporary wharf, for the purpose of embarking the troops to pass them over to the opposite shore, where the enemy's forces appeared to muster strongly. I was informed that the materials intended for this purpose would be found in the fort. I arrived at my destination at the first peep of dawn, and commenced an active search and earnest inquiries after the requisite necessaries to enable us to commence operations: not a plank or piece of timber of any description was forthcoming. The boat, after landing us, had immediately returned to the Plover, so that I had no opportunity of communicating the impossibility of executing my orders. While idling about with my people waiting for the first boat to make known my situation, Colonel B—d—yl, of the Guards, a near relation of one of our lieutenants, arrived at Bathz; and after exchanging the ordinary salutations, very kindly and hospitably requested me to accompany him to his quarters, an excellent farmhouse in the neighbourhood, to breakfast. I pleaded being on duty. "But there is no duty to perform," said he; "come along, it is close by: besides, is it not wise to be prepared for work when it does come?"

I foolishly suffered myself to be beguiled by the tempting offer, and accompanied the soldier. The "close by," (which to a mounted man might appear so,) proved to be three miles. The breakfast was excellent, and the conversation so agreeable that the time slipped away imperceptibly. I was startled at finding two hours had elapsed since my departure from my party. I scampered back as fast as my legs would carry me, but, alas! I had the mortification to find that the Commodore had already been there, the whole of the working-party taken off,—his compliments left for me, and, when I was tired of my inland cruise, I might repair on board again. There I sauntered all day with the most humiliating feelings, conscious that I had deeply and deservedly offended my commanding officer by the acceptance of an invitation frankly and hospitably tendered, but which I ought to have at once positively declined.

Sunset came before I could obtain a passage on board the Plover. The Commodore was at dinner; I waited in anxious trepidation the conclusion of the repast. The captain came on deck, I reported myself. "I am sorry for you, S—, but the Commodore is extremely angry, has desired me to say that he has no further occasion for your services, and has ordered me to send you back to the Belleisle by the first opportunity."

I bowed in silence, and retired. Immediately afterwards, my friend W—p—l, our first lieutenant, accosted me: " What a d—d fool you are, Master Jemmy, — always getting yourself into a scrape about the shore! You are to be sent back to the ship." I explained to him the particulars. " It will be of no avail, I fear; he appears determined to punish you by sending you to the rear."

My reflections were bitter and overpowering, and I resolved to request that I might be discharged from the service, although I had that day completed my six years' probation. While this was passing in my mind, Captain B—n again ascended the deck, having reported my return to the Commodore. " Mr. S. the Commodore wishes to see you in the cabin," was the startling announcement; I descended with the full conviction that my fate was sealed, and had worked my courage up to the sticking-place, to put forth a request to leave the service, as soon as I should receive the order for my dismissal to the rear.

On opening the cabin-door, I scarcely knew whether the power of hearing was not suddenly inverted by some of those malicious sprites who delight in sporting with the miseries of mortals, when I heard myself addressed without the ceremonious *Mr.* tacked to my name, a custom by which I could always distinguish how I stood in the Commodore's opinion at the moment of address. When my surname was simply made use of, all was right; but the handle of *Mr.* ever sounded ominous, and jarred on my auditory nerves. It may be supposed that this unexpected salutation threw me most agreeably aback; but the fear that it was only the prelude to a less harsh but more cutting reprimand kept me in suspense for some seconds. The gloomy atmosphere which enveloped my prospects as I entered the cabin cleared away, and a sunshine so flattering to my hopes and dazzling to my ambition burst upon me, that I could scarcely credit the sudden revulsion of feeling that assailed me. No rebuke,—not an allusion to my unlucky breakfast cruise was breathed, but addressing me in that gratifying style of communication he always assumed when delivering his orders upon service against the enemy, he continued, "S—, the Commander-in-chief has desired me to fix upon an officer in whom I can place confidence to entrust with a particular service this night, and he has authorized me to state to the officer selected, that, should he succeed in the performance of the prescribed duty, he shall receive his commission to-morrow. I have named you ;—be prepared at nine o'clock, when I will give you the necessary orders."

Whether I stood upon my head or my heels was at that moment a matter of doubt to me; my ideas were so confused, and suffered such a complete bewilderment, that my utterance was choked, and I was obliged to pause ere my feelings would permit me to express my thanks for the confidence bestowed upon me. To be suddenly recalled, as it appeared to me, from banishment, and placed in a fair way to obtain honourable promotion, was the *summum bonum* of happiness, beyond all that I could have imagined or aspired to. Need I declare the lasting impression the events of that day made upon me? I descended into the gun-room, where the officers had hospitably invited me to mess during the time the Commodore's broad pendant was flying.

At the appointed hour I received my orders, and left the ship. I fortunately succeeded in executing my instructions, and the next day I was in possession of a letter from Sir Richard Keats, enclosing another from the Commander-in-chief with an acting commission, appointing me to the Resolution, seventy-four, in the vacancy of Lieutenant R—, who had been killed. So true it is, the shot that lays one low elevates another!

Through the friendly representations of the Commodore I was placed in command of one of the gun-boats under his orders, instead of joining the Resolution, then lying in the Roompot. The unfortunate circumstances which produced a cessation of further hostilities caused us to retrograde down the Scheldt. Off Flushing I was attacked with the malignant fever which carried off so many thousands of our countrymen, and I removed on board the Commodore; and shortly after the Belleisle was ordered home. The boat I had commanded having been lost a few days subsequently to my quitting her, Commodore C. took me home with him to England.

Weeks elapsed before I was enabled to appear

at the bar of the big-wigs at Somerset House, assembled monthly to examine into the qualifications of young naval aspirants. The middy's buttons replaced the acting lieutenant's on my coat for this occasion. I was so absorbed with my own pressing affairs that I little heeded the many anxious faces around me; but I well remember one poor fellow, who, (with all the confidence that a knowledge of John Hamilton Moore by rote could well inspire,) ascended the stairs with the tread of conscious superiority, and again made his appearance in the hall with melancholy step and slow: the young heroes crowded around their hapless brother, overpowering him with questions as to the result and mode of his categorical ordeal; he burst into tears, rushed from the hall, and made a bolt through the quadrangle as if pursued by a legion of devils. I was one of the fortunate who came off with flying colours; but whether proceeding from excitation of mind, acting upon a scarcely convalescent frame, or from some less remote cause, I had a dangerous attack during the night, which ended in a pleuritic fever. This unfortunate illness delayed for some time my receipt and the deposit of my passing certificate at the Admiralty; but when that preliminary step was adopted, and a representation made in my favour by Captain C—, I was confirmed in my rank, and ordered to join the Resolution. But I then lay in a deplorable state, and a certificate from Astley Cooper brought my discharge, and an order to report myself when ready for service again. For three months my life was not worth a day's purchase; a relapse had rendered matters worse, and I began to fear I should never more sport a lieutenant's uniform: the miseries of the Walcheren fever were submerged in the more violent malady that consumed my strength and energies.

As soon as I considered myself sufficiently strong, I put Astley Cooper's mandate aside, and reported myself to their Lordships as fit for sea. By return of post I found myself nominated to his Majesty's ship F—che, " willing and requiring me forthwith to repair on board, and to take upon me the charge and command of lieutenant accordingly."

I proceeded to the Downs, but she had sailed to Sheerness, where I joined her, and to my astonishment found I was first lieutenant. The vessel requiring to be docked, we were ordered into the harbour. A short time elapsed when the acting lieutenant was superseded by one senior to myself, and I was speedily shorn of my responsibility. Unfortunately, the Commander and the newly appointed officer did not suit each other; the harmony that subsisted between the gun-room and the captain was consequently interrupted, and produced a state of things incompatible with the good discipline of the ship. There were, undoubtedly, faults on both sides, but the course adopted by the gun-room was highly reprehensible, and in no way to be excused by the cause of offence.

The dock-yard at Sheerness was so occupied with the refitment of numerous vessels, that we were despatched to Northfleet to be docked in a merchant's yard. In consequence of no hulk being provided for the ship's company, they were retained on board. The Commander, on quitting the dock-yard in the afternoon, left orders with the first lieutenant, that he was to send all of them on board the Rodney, seventy-four, lying in the river, which had just come down from Woolwich. Accordingly, I was despatched with a party of them; but the commanding officer of the Rodney, having had no orders on the subject, refused to receive them, and I had to return with the men. Messages passed between the two first lieutenants, but, the senior officer adhering to his first refusal, the ship's company remained on board.

At seven bells in the first watch, the captain returned on board. Mr. T—t had remained up to that late hour for the purpose of explaining the reason of his not having been enabled to comply with the orders he had received. "But why did not you send on board again, Mr. T. ?"—"I did, sir, but the refusal was repeated."—"But why did you not send again?" reiterated the Captain.—"How, sir, after I had been twice answered!"—"Yes, sir, you ought to have repeated my orders." — The patience of the lieutenant was exhausted by these querulous questions, and he answered (improperly)—"Good G— ! sir, would you have had me act like a d—d fool ?"—"Have you act like a d—d fool ?" repeated the astounded skipper in amaze—"Sentry," addressing the marine, " take notice of what this officer says —Did you hear what has just passed ?"—" Yes, sir." Mr. T. was immediately placed under an arrest, and I again carried on the duty. All my endeavours to prevent a court martial were ineffectual : a too high demand on one side, and an unflinching determination to abide the decision of the court on the other, marred all my attempts at reconciliation. My great object now was to quit the ship, and, having obtained permission to write to be superseded, my request was assented to by return of post, and three months allowed me to remain on shore to recover my health, which continued terribly shaken.

I was most sadly perplexed and annoyed, on communicating the intelligence to the Captain, to find that my expectations of release were postponed *sine die*, by his declaring he was determined to detain me as a witness against my messmate. On our return to Sheerness, the court martial was held on board the old Magnanime.

Of all the disagreeable events that occur in his Majesty's service, certainly courts martial stand pre-eminent on the list of vexations. A court martial should at all times be an ungrateful task to prosecutors, even when based upon public duty; but when other and private feelings, inimical to the true interests of the service, prompt men to search out and provoke a breach of discipline in order to further their unworthy intentions, the offender may be pronounced as more sinned against than sinning, and the prosecutor must lose in the estimation of every well-wisher to the military professions.

My evidence having been given, the sentry, who was supposed to have heard the conversation between the two officers, was called before the court. After taking the usual oath, the witness was desired to state all that he knew; the man fidgeted, hemmed and hawed, without uttering a sentence.

Prosecutor.—" You were on duty as sentry the first watch when I returned on board the day we were docked?"—" Yes, sir."

Pros.—" You heard what passed between Lieutenant T. and myself that evening?"—" Yes, sir."

" You remember perfectly all that occurred?" —" Oh yes, sir."

"Then relate to the court all you know."—
"Yes, sir."—A long pause.

"Well, begin." — "I remember you called Lieutenant T. a d—d fool, sir."—All the members looked up in astonishment.

Pros.—"Do you mean to swear that?"— "Yes, sir."

Pros.—"Do you know you have taken a solemn oath to speak the truth, and nothing but the truth?"—"Oh yes, sir, I know I have; I should be sorry to forswear myself. I remember perfectly well, as if it only happened this moment, you called Lieutenant T. a d—d fool."

The poor marine was questioned and cross-questioned in every possible way; nothing could be drawn from him to shake his testimony; and the evidence for the prosecution closed. The verdict of acquittal was pronounced, accompanied by a caution to be more careful for the future.

The fact was, the witness had not heard the lieutenant's speech addressed to the captain, and only caught the repetition of it by the latter, as they were in the act of turning round; and it was impressed on his mind that the skipper alone had made use of the obnoxious observation. Be it as it may, the decided manner in which he delivered his evidence went far to do away with the heavy charge brought against the lieutenant; and he escaped, as I have mentioned.

I joyfully bade adieu to La F——che, for every thing on board was so totally at variance with all I had been accustomed to, that I believe I should have rather returned to the middy's berth with my former captain, than have remained where I was as a lieutenant. Dame Fortune certainly interposed her good offices in my favour on this occasion. Scarcely had a week passed before La F——che was totally wrecked on the coast of Holland. This was the second time I had narrowly escaped experiencing the miseries of shipwreck upon an enemy's coast.

I returned home, and thence proceeded to Brighton for the re-establishment of my health. Before the expiration of the stipulated three months, my anxiety to get afloat again led me to report myself ready for sea.

I was appointed to the Myrtle, a frigate sloop, then at Lisbon, and was at the same time ordered to Portsmouth for a passage on board the Goshawk, Captain Lilburn.

I found Captain Charles Napier as a fellow-passenger, who was an inmate of Barbadoes Hospital during the time I lay ill there with the fever, and who there visited me hourly, to observe the rapid decay of the human frame under the influence of that consuming disease. He was going out as an amateur, to witness the exploits of our army. When we arrived off Oporto we heard that Lord Wellington had commenced a retrograde movement before the overwhelming force of Massena. Captain Napier left us at that place, and succeeded in joining the British forces in time to be present at the battle of Busaco, and to get hit. This enterprising officer has been wounded many times.*

On my arrival at Lisbon, I was turned over to the Barfleur, to await the return of the Myrtle. I was here introduced to a knot of most excellent fellows, for many of whom I still feel the liveliest interest and regard. The ward-room mess of the Barfleur was arranged with scrupulous nicety and

* The present admiral of the Portuguese fleet.

punctuality. It might have served as a model for the imitation of the navy at large. The mess had a numerous military acquaintance, and, two days in the week being set apart for public occasions, each member was allowed to invite his friends, on paying a moderate sum into the common fund towards the extra expenses incurred. These reunions of red and blue coats were delightful, and certainly formed the most agreeable mess parties on ship-board I have ever met with. The best band in the navy, composed entirely of Germans, (formerly the Dutch Admiral de Winter's,) increased our pleasure by their performances; the hilarity of the company was uninterrupted; no excess was ever committed, and hosts and guests always separated from each other with regret.

As a supernumerary lieutenant I was a most independent person, and merrily did I profit by my state of freedom. I was introduced by my messmates to several Portuguese families, with whom I kept up an acquaintance during the time I remained upon the station, particularly that of the M‑ch‑re‑as.

No sea-approach can be finer than that which

conducts you to Lisbon. Passing between the Catchops, two dangerous sands, you enter the mouth of the beautiful estuary, defended on one side by the castle of St. Julian, and on the other by the Bugio, a small fort built on the sands, which in bad weather appears to be almost smothered by the heavy sea that breaks at its base, the spray flying over it in foaming sheets of water.

The sail from the Bugio to the Torre de Belem, with the appearance of the city standing upon a succession of hills running along the banks of the river, is beautiful; the climate is soft and salubrious; and the stranger is plunged into a chaos of delicious sensations as he views the rich and variegated picture spread before him. But here the pleasing panorama ends. The town abounds in ill-paved streets and steep ascents; heaps of filth and abomination, disgusting to the eye and offensive to the smell, occupy both sides and every corner; the houses, originally white, are so bespattered and bedaubed, that the mind sickens at the sight of what in the distance wears so alluring and captivating an aspect. The shops are equally ill-arranged and filthy; those in the best quarter, Gold, Silver, and Cloth Streets, may perhaps be pronounced a degree better than their neighbours. In fact, those streets, leading into the square of the Inquisition, were the only places we could walk in with any hope of comfort or security from the detestable Portuguese habit of throwing every species of filth out of their windows.

It is a matter of considerable surprise that the total absence of cleanliness in Lisbon does not engender a succession of dreadful maladies. It is a fortunate circumstance for the inhabitants that the site of the city was laid upon hills, or they would certainly be buried in their own filth. The heavy rains wash the accumulation of dirt to the base of the hills, where it becomes a formidable barrier until the impetuous rushing of the waters in a heavy storm of rain breaks through the dam of corruption, and carries the whole into the river.

At the time of my arrival, the Tagus was filled with men-of-war and transports; great numbers of the latter were moored in the large bay above the dock-yard. On the approach of Lord Wellington towards Lisbon, the transports in the latter position were ordered down to Belem. This movement created considerable alarm to a great majority of the Portuguese, who regarded it as a prelude to the evacuation of the city. The news of the battle of Busaco did not elevate their hopes, as it was known the army still continued its retreat. The account of this brilliant affair invigorated the spirits of every Englishman, and the successful stand at the lines was predicted with all the confidence which the genius and abilities of the British chief warranted. People were, however, on the *qui vive* as the army approached nearer to Lisbon. Everything that might prove in any way useful to the invaders was swept away before the retreating force.

The crowds of peasantry that made their way to the capital from the country, flying from their foes, accumulated as the enemy closed in upon the environs of the city: the distress of many was pitiable; they had left all behind them, and were literally without any support but the casual benevolence of a few, who had so many calls upon their humanity that their means were speedily exhausted. Many of great respectability were reduced to the extremity of begging of our countrymen : it was melancholy to witness well-dressed Portuguese watching the opportunity of whispering their tales of distress, and petitions for aid, in the ears of the English, hoping to escape the observation of the passers by, and their own country people. The man who could resist the appeal of interesting females, the withering look of agony and humiliation which marked their countenances, as they implored relief for some cherished object perishing with hunger and misery, must have been made of sterner stuff than usually forms the component parts of our nature.

The calamities of the inhabitants of a country exposed to war are severe ; friends and foes must alike be provided for, and all the means in their possession are relentlessly demanded, and carried off; any hesitation or refusal only subjects them to rougher treatment and exactions.

Lisbon was full to overflowing with the unfortunate refugees; there was not house-room for the poor wretches, and many had to fight with the mongrel curs that swarmed the streets for their lairs on the quays, and wherever the smallest shelter could be obtained : the sight was truly distressing.

The numerous frightful objects exposed at certain intervals on the highways, to excite the commiseration of the passengers, are too horrible to describe. It might be supposed that Lisbon was a receptacle for the most revolting afflictions to which " flesh is heir." It required no long residence to enable me to perceive what class in this unhappy country lived upon the fat of the land; the numerous good-looking, sleek, broad-shouldered adherents of Mother Church, to be met with in every part of the town, would alone proclaim the fact, that the bosom of the Catholic faith had the will and the power of cherishing her faithful servants. The gorgeous trappings and costly ornaments in the interior of the churches evinced their industry and success in impressing upon the minds of their flocks the necessity of contributing —largely contributing to the splendour of their religion. The French, by the by, took no trifling liberties with the goods and chattels belonging to the godly fathers. They attempted to remove the superb mosaics from St. Roque's, but desisted from their object on finding the safe removal of them impracticable : the injury would have been so serious as to render them valueless.

Politic as Napoleon's conduct generally was towards the countries that fell under his sway, it is extraordinary that he took no measures to propitiate the priesthood of countries so bigoted as those of Spain and Portugal : whatever opposition his troops met with from the peasantry, may be traced to the steady enmity of the holy orders towards a change of dynasty promising a different state of things, at once inimical to their temporal interests and spiritual power. The priesthood took especial care to inculcate the spirit of enmity into the minds of their followers, the seed sown prospered and blossomed, and they are now reaping a rich harvest of tyranny and bigotry.

On visiting the Cathedral with some friends, the mark of a cross deeply indented (as if done by a finger) in the stone at the foot of a staircase attracted my attention; it was explained by our cicerone. We were gravely assured it was performed by St. Anthony with his forefinger, when his Satanic Majesty attended upon his footsteps, tempting him to err: the holy symbol of our religion arrested the progress of the arch deceiver and prince of darkness, and St. Anthony escaped further persecution by ascending the stairs. The smile of incredulity which played upon the faces of our party was not unobserved by the good man who expounded the miracle, and we sank accordingly in his estimation.

The next objects that invited our curiosity were two ravens; these wonderful and longevous birds had two hundred and fifty years before miraculously conducted a vessel into the harbour of Lisbon, without a living thing on board but themselves. When we ventured to express a doubt of their being the identical birds that had proved themselves such skilful pilots, our pious and credulous conductor lost all patience with the unbelieving heretics, and, without waiting for the fee usually tendered by our countrymen on such occasions, abruptly quitted us; we therefore pursued our investigations without the aid of his legendary lore.

In winding our course through the galleries under the body of the church appropriated to the dead, I observed the figure of a child, dressed in the most gaudy but rich attire, lying upon a bier: the light was dim, and I supposed it to be a wax figure placed there as a *memento mori* by the holy fathers for the admiration of visitors. I was dwelling upon the beauty of the work, and its faithful resemblance to a dead child, when one of my companions, who had been long stationed at Lisbon, assured me it was no counterfeit, but *bona fide* a corpse. I was incredulous until I placed my hand upon the face: the chilling contact convinced me of the fact.

I found that, when the parents or friends of the deceased were so poor as to be unable to pay the burial expenses, it was the custom for the parents to take the body to the monks, who dressed and exposed it to public view, until the pious donations of the visitors to the church should amount to the requisite sum to induce the reverend fathers of the establishment to pay the last sad rites to their fellow mortal.

The numerous black crosses to be seen placed against the houses naturally drew forth an inquiry as to their origin and meaning. The stranger is astonished to find that each declares a murder to have been committed in the house or near the spot. I should hope that some of them were of many years' standing, or the deeds of blood that occur in that capital must be of fearful amount.

During my first visit to Lisbon a murderer was executed, his head cut off, and stuck on a pole by the arsenal wall, opposite to the house where the crime was committed, and in one of the most public and frequented streets of the town. The spectacle was as disgusting and horrid as the imagination can well conceive: there was no assembly of the people; it appeared an affair not worthy of notice. On passing the spot near midnight, the only individuals I perceived in the street were some of my countrymen collected around the pole: they were all of the medical department; their zeal for the practical part of their profession had determined them to walk off with the exposed head of the murderer. I presume they effected their object, for the police were not a little surprised the following morning to find the pole divested of its head ornament.

The arrival of the Myrtle ended my shore excursions. I joined my new ship, and found myself first lieutenant. It had been announced to me that I was to fill that post on my arrival on board the Barfleur, but it was an arrangement I had not expected on quitting England, and it therefore proved to me doubly welcome. These frigate-built vessels were rated at eighteen guns, but mounted twenty-six.

This class of vessels has very wisely been done away with; few of them were capable of performing any other service than that of keeping company with convoys. On the score of comfort and accommodation to the officers and ship's company they far exceeded the brigs; but, in my opinion, there must have been a great deficiency of nautical taste on the part of the man who could have preferred the first to the latter enviable description of vessels. The eighteen gun-brigs could both fight and run;—the ship sloops were scarcely able to perform the most essential part of their duty in blowing hard weather; as for running, they were about as capable of such a feat as the old cow. The jackass frigates of the present day (as they are generally denominated) are certainly first cousins on both sides to the late ship sloops.

My commander, Captain Cowan, had been first lieutenant of the Barfleur, and was now acting in the absence of Captain I—s. He was an old officer, had been constantly at sea, and had long filled the responsible situation of first lieutenant in a line-of-battle ship, equally to the credit of himself, and to the comfort of all placed under him. Captain Hall, in his " Fragments," has so justly and faithfully portrayed the character of this excellent officer, that any attempt of mine to do justice to his merits would be superfluous.

CHAPTER IX.

Trip to Cadiz—The French open a fire on us—Touch at Gibraltar—Proceed to Algiers—Our Jewish friend—A Dispute—Bathing—Fidelity and sagacity of a Newfoundland Dog—Return to Lisbon—A bereaved Family—Trial for High Treason—Terrible Execution.

Our first trip was to Cadiz, for dollars. Capt. Cowan astonished me not a little by observing that he had never witnessed a shot fired in anger during the whole of his active career. I forget the number of years it embraced, but the singular part of the business was, that he had been constantly in sea-going ships, ever in search of enemies, and had never encountered any capable of resistance. Yet how far more deserving of promotion was this officer than the many who, with not a third part of his knowledge and abilities, had by mere good luck been so placed and circumstanced as to enable them to push their claims with success. The service is a lottery in this respect: it was the fate of Captain Cowan to experience all the real fag and hardships of the profession without receiving an adequate reward.

Cadiz formed a pleasing and striking contrast to Lisbon in the cleanliness and neatness of its streets. My observations were limited to an hour's excursion on shore; but this hurried *coup-d'œil* created an anxious desire to see more of it, which was at a later period amply gratified. Soult was then laying siege to Cadiz, but, except the occasional interchange of shot and shell between the gun-boats and bomb-vessels and the French batteries, I saw little that reminded me of a besieged town. The mortars by which he was enabled to throw the shells to so much greater a distance than we had been accustomed to imagine possible, were not then in battery.

Having taken our freight on board, we weighed with a beating wind. Standing too close to Fort Catalina, and the wind suddenly failing us, the Frenchmen opened out upon us. Here, then, was the first time that Captain Cowan ever came under the fire of the enemy.

Cooped up within the lines of Torres Vedras, and shut out from receiving any supplies from the interior, the army had to receive, as well as Lisbon itself, all supplies from without. The Alentejo and the Algarves certainly were open, but the products bore no proportion to the immense consumption. The Americans supplied the principal part of the corn and flour, but on the first commencement of Massena's blockade it did not equal the demands: Captain Cowan was therefore despatched with a convoy of transports to the Barbary coast, for the purpose of procuring a sufficient quantity of corn.

We touched at Gibraltar: it was the first time I had entered the Straits, and I could not but be forcibly struck by the novelty of the scene before me. The frowning and impregnable rock itself has been so often and so accurately described, that it would be an intrusion to introduce it here.

We took our departure from the Pillars of Hercules with the convoy, and proceeded to Algiers, the first port at which we intended to commence marketing. A visit to that stronghold was then considered a great novelty, but it has lost much of its interest now from being occupied by Europeans. Its situation upon the side of a hill, the houses rising one above the other, and their dead walls, (for not a window is to be seen,) give it a singular and sombre appearance. The houses are quadrangular, with a court in the middle, into which the apartments look. The streets, if alleys can be so styled, are extremely narrow. The tops of the houses incline towards each other, and nearly meet, so that the inhabitants can with facility step from one roof to another: they are flat, and form a promenade for their females. We met a few women in the streets, but they appeared to be of the lowest class; had their stature corresponded with their one-eyed appearance, one might have taken them for the Cyclops of old.

We were treated with much civility, indeed I may add marked attention, by the admiral and some of the higher officers. Not obtaining a sufficient store of supplies, we departed for Bona with the unloaded part of our convoy; and by the assistance of a rich Algerine Jew, whom we took on board at Algiers, we succeeded in our object. On our return we hove-to in Algiers bay to land our Jewish friend. It was late in the afternoon: the boat had scarcely got within the mole-head, when the weather became so boisterous that the ship was obliged to stand out to sea. The officer, anxious to get on board, pushed out. Darkness came on, and she lay exposed to the inclemency of the weather all night. At daylight she bore up for the harbour, where, on landing, the Algerine Admiral met them. He immediately gave orders for the accommodation and refreshment of the crew; had the pinnace hauled up by his own people; issued the strictest orders that care should be taken of every thing, and, taking the officer to his own habitation, bestowed every friendly attention upon him. The lieutenant was highly gratified; he set him down as a right hearty good fellow; but the flowing current of his good opinion was suddenly arrested by the fierce look, curling mustachios, and deadly threat held out by the potent bashaw to an unfortunate Portuguese slave, who, in handing some coffee to the guest, accidentally spilt it over him. The poor wretch trembled like an aspen leaf at his master's anger.

The next day the weather moderating, the ship stood in and picked up the pinnace. A Portuguese sloop of war, placed under our orders, was despatched with the loaded vessels, to convoy them to Gibraltar, where we were to rejoin them. From Algiers we proceeded to Oran, and anchored under the walls of Marselquiver Castle, the fortifications of which appeared in a very dilapidated state. We were saluted on our arrival, and the compliment was duly returned.

We were at dinner in the captain's cabin, when an Algerine officer from the castle came on board, to demand a certain number of barrels of gunpowder, as an indemnification for the salute given us, which indemnification would have amounted to about twenty times the amount expended by the attentive commandant. The envoy was ushered into the cabin, and communicated to the captain himself the purport of his visit: he was politely informed that it was not usual with British men-of-war to submit to such demands, consequently his could not be complied with. When the answer was made known to the Turk through his interpreter, his countenance expressed astonishment and anger at the audacity of the Christian dogs; he gave vent to his indignation in a rhapsody of unintelligible jargon; and intimated his determination not to quit the ship till the demand was complied with. While we sipped our wine, the indignant Moslem seated himself upon one of the guns, but, observing that his threats and anger were alike unheeded, he abruptly left us, saying, if the powder was not immediately sent on shore, he would sink us. "Just as you please," answered the captain; "but, remember, two can play at that game." The guns in the dilapidated castle remained silent; but the next day, when we were embarking our stock at Oran, an order suddenly arrived from the Bey that nothing was to be taken off. The English vice-consul immediately interfered, but the mighty man could not be appeased, and we received a hint that the sooner we got off to our ship the better. The dispute terminated by our being obliged to embark the consul and his family, and leave a port where we had experienced a reception so totally different from that at Algiers. The arms of Spain are still seen over the different gateways, and the place appears to have been formerly one of great strength, but I imagine the adjoining hills completely command it.

We found the Portuguese sloop with our convoy awaiting us at Gibraltar, whence we took our departure at the first spirt of easterly wind for the Tagus; on our arrival at the latter place, Captain Cowan was superseded by Captain S—yd.

Whenever the weather would permit, the ship's company were allowed to bathe alongside, in a sail suspended from the fore and main yard-arms. We had on board a valuable Newfoundland dog of great size: Boatswain was not only the pet and delight of the middies' berth, but equally enjoyed the goodwill of the whole crew; the animal richly merited the affection and attentions showered upon him. His station, while the men were sporting in the water, was always on the gangway, couchant, with his fore paws over the gunnel, and his head so far advanced that he could obtain a clear view of all that was passing under him.

Did the cry for assistance reach his ear, Boatswain would instantly distinguish it from amidst the hubbub of the multitude, prick up his ears, jump overboard, and swim to the person who appeared to require his assistance. Though fond of the water, he could never be prevailed upon to join his shipmates in this luxury; it would seem as. if he constituted himself guardian of the bathers, watching their movements with the fidelity and anxiety of an old servant for the safety of his master's children.

A marine who had just joined the ship, and who was unacquainted with the excellent qualities of the dog, endeavoured while bathing to entice him from his station into the water; the noble animal paid no attention to his invitation. One of the crew told the marine, that if he swam out of the sail, and would call out as if in distress, and suit the action to the word, Mr. Boatswain would certainly obey his summons. The marine took the hint, got out of the sail, and began to enact the part of a drowning man to perfection. The dog instantly sprang into the water, with his ears erect, his eyes flashing fire, from intense anxiety;

away he swam for the soldier, who, on the approach of his canine friend, began to have some misgivings as to the wisdom of his proceedings. He now became alarmed, lest the dog should seize him, which manœuvre Boatswain appeared resolved to execute: his fears increased with the dog's endeavours to effect his purpose; and finally, he roared out most lustily for help from his shipmates. The louder the poor devil sang out, the more determined was the sagacious brute to seize him; and he very soon accomplished his purpose, grasping him firmly by the hair at the back of the neck, and, twisting his face towards the heavens, brought him alongside, amidst the convulsive roars of laughter of the whole of the ship's company, and the piteous cries of the jolly marine. Boatswain would not resign his hold till the frightened man was assisted up the side; the bight of a rope being then placed overboard for his conductor, he placed his fore-legs in it up to his shoulders, and, holding himself stiffly out, was hauled up, and calmly resumed his watch as if nothing had happened.— This noble quadruped had saved several lives. Whilst lying in

Hamoaze, a shore-boat pulling athwart the ship's hawse in a strong ebb tide, took the cable amid ships, and was upset: he was overboard in a moment, and succeeded in saving a woman and a man.

Whenever the ship's company were exercised at the guns with blank cartridge, or at the target, the dog was at the acme of delight and ecstacy; he appeared mad with enjoyment, running and jumping from one gun to another, as they were fired. When corporal punishment took place, he was the veriest picture of gravity that can be imagined; placing himself in the centre of the vacant part of the deck immediately before the upright gratings, and watching with solemn interest the whole proceedings. Not so if any irregular disturbance occurred among the people themselves. Three men were quarrelling one day and came to blows before the master-at-arms could interfere; the animal was attracted to the spot by the uproar, and, not understanding this mode of settling disputes, immediately brought one of the combatants to the deck, and separated the other two, with the most perfect coolness of purpose. Boatswain appeared thoroughly to understand the discipline of a man-of-war, and never permitted anything like fighting to go on without attacking the parties. The officers and crew derived great amusement from the equestrian feats of a middy (eleven or twelve years old, but extremely small for his age,) who, mounted upon the back of the gallant dog, would gallop helter-skelter round the decks. This racing, however, was forbidden, in consequence of considerable danger attending it: the dog one day made a sudden leap with his rider from the quarter-deck on to the main; I fortunately saved the lad's head from coming in contact with one of the iron belaying-pins fixed into the skids. Dogs are generally great nuisances on board a ship, but the Newfoundland race may be excepted, and often form a valuable acquisition; I however fear there are few who could compete with our old favourite.

Our next arrival at Cadiz was just at the period of the battle of Barossa, and the operations against the enemy's works in the bay. This brilliant achievement of the army did not perhaps insure all the advantages to be anticipated from such an event, in consequence of the pusillanimous conduct of the Spanish troops, but it afforded another proof of the sterling powers of British soldiers.

On our return to Lisbon I visited the M—cha—as family, ranking as one of the first in birth and fortune among the Portuguese nobility. The head of this noble house had, for some political reasons, been sent out of the kingdom; and it was currently reported and universally believed that the eldest son had entered the service of France, and was acting as aid-de-camp to one of the French marshals. The lady mother and three of her daughters remained in Lisbon at the imminent hazard of their lives; so enraged were their countrymen against all the members of a family, the males of which they considered as traitors to their country. Twice indeed the irritation of the mob excited fears for their safety, and the military were called in to protect them from their fury. In all my conversations with the young ladies they appeared to feel acutely the rash action of which their brother had been guilty. Regarding them as meritorious and unprotected females exposed to the insults of a ruffianly rabble, I felt much interested for them, and frequently visited the sombre palace of the unfortunate M—cha—as, in preference to the gay parties of their happier compatriots. The tranquillity of our small party was sadly interrupted one evening, by a servant announcing to his lady that he had heard his young master was taken and on his way to Lisbon. All was dismay and agony—I took my departure, having first promised (at the request of the elder sister) to use my best endeavours to ascertain the truth of the statement, and to call upon them the following day with the result of my inquiries.

I very soon learned the melancholy certainty of their misery; the young man had been taken in the disguise of a peasant, conveying French despatches across the country. In two days he was expected in Lisbon, to take his trial for high treason.

I absolutely quailed under the task imposed upon me, to be the bearer of such agonizing tidings—to lacerate the heart of the mother piecemeal as I unfolded the dreadful truth of her son's undoing—the dishonour of the heir of her ancient race and name ; not a glimmering of hope, not a ray of consolation dared I offer to soften the calamity that had fallen upon this bereaved family.

I entered the gloomy mansion. Three young females, pale as the angel of death, rushed towards me, grasped my hands, and with quivering lips vainly essayed to ask the fatal question. The mother — But what boots it now to tell of agony passed, of hope destroyed—of the deadly throes of the bitterest of all human bitterness? My tale was told—the iron entered into their souls—the proud house of M–cha–as was humbled to the dust—I never saw them again.

*   *   *   *

They denied themselves to all inquiries, and dedicated the energies of their minds to ward off the dreadful fate that hung over the misguided son and brother. The interest, the entreaties, the heart-rending petitions employed by these stricken beings, failed in their effects. M–cha–as was doomed to die. The heads of the government were resolutely determined that he should suffer the extreme penalty of the law. The young man confronted his accusers and judges with dignity, defending his conduct with the specious enthusiasm to be expected from a young and ardent admirer of the great captain of the age, in whose service he had enrolled himself. He had adopted the idea that a connection with France would prove more beneficial to his country than an alliance with England; but, in his admiration for Napoleon, he had overlooked the duty which every man owes to his native soil.

When sentence was pronounced, he threatened his judges with the vengeance of his master, the great Napoleon, and denied their power and authority to try or condemn him; and in this frame of mind he remained till within a day of his execution, when he suddenly acknowledged the guilt and folly of his conduct, and received the religious consolations tendered to him by his church: he had previously rejected all communication with the priesthood. The place wherein he was to expiate his errors with his life, bore the name of Berkeley Square among the English; I forget its Portuguese appellation. One side of this square was formed by the quay on the river; Arsenal Street ran parallel with the Tagus on the opposite side. In the centre of the square, a circular scaffold was erected eight or ten feet high, in the middle of which rose a stout spar five feet above the platform. To the spar was affixed a seat on which the culprit was to sit; the planks were laid five or six inches apart from each other, and were very narrow; the whole of the under part was filled up with faggots, plentifully interspersed with inflammable matter.

Few events could have created a greater sensation among the inhabitants of every grade in Lisbon, than the condemnation and approaching execution of one of their highest nobles. It may be supposed that his numerous friends and relatives left no means untried to avert the dreadful sentence; many of his own rank in life, though completely at variance with the political tenets of the unfortunate prisoner, joined in the prayer of the supplicants,—I believe more from the feeling of disgrace thrown upon their order, than from any friendly solicitude towards him or his family. But among the middle and lower classes not a voice was raised in his favour. Had mercy been shown towards him, it is not improbable that an insurrectionary movement would have taken place.

All these circumstances, of course, had their due weight and consideration with the ruling powers; besides, in the then existing state of the country, the necessity of making a severe example of so conspicuous an offender was obvious. The decree was confirmed, and the day fixed for his execution.

I was one of the English officers who witnessed the awful spectacle: we repaired to the spot about ten o'clock in the morning. That side of the square facing the river was left open, the other three were lined with troops three deep, close up to the houses; around the scaffold was another body of troops, forming a small circle not thirty feet from the faggots. No person was allowed to enter this reserved circle but the English officers, and a very few natives of the higher orders. All the houses that could command a view of the spot were crowded from the roof downwards; they presented one mass of human beings packed almost to suffocation. The windows were studded with heads from the sills to the uppermost parts. The whole line through which the cavalcade passed exhibited the same anxious solicitude to catch a glimpse of the condemned. The shipping in the river, from the fishing-boat to the largest vessel, in the line of view, were clustered like bees from the truck to the deck, on the rigging, yards, and spars. The eager gaze and indistinct hum of those who commanded a view of Arsenal Street, announced that the procession had entered it. All was hushed; the melancholy tinkling of the bell belonging to the Host, which accompanied the *cortège*, was alone heard in the distance, gradually increasing, until, with the measured tramp of human footsteps, it became more painfully audible.

The banners of the monks were seen waving over the bayonets of the troops. Suddenly the latter opened their ranks to the right and left, and the principal personage in the melancholy drama appeared, clothed in a loose white dress, bare-footed, carrying a cross upon his right shoulder. A high paper cap, bearing the inscription of "Traitor!" covered his head. I can never forget the convulsive start, the look of horror that spread over his fine features as the scaffold broke abruptly on his view. Even at this dreadful moment, and under other circumstances, I should have recognised him by the striking resemblance he bore to his elder sister. He rallied and walked on to the foot of the fatal steps that were to conduct him to eternity. Here he remained in prayer for a short time with the monks around him. The last rites administered, the cross was taken from his shoulder, and, bidding farewell to his ghostly advisers, he ascended the scaffold, attended by one of the friars. He tripped at the first step, but, immediately recovering himself, mounted with a firm and resolute bearing. Here again for a short time he entered into earnest conversation with his religious attendant. He then submitted himself to the hands of the executioner, by sitting down on the seat I have described, with his back to the stout spar, against which his head reclined; his hands were then lashed together before him, and his legs to the uprights that supported the seat. The paper cap was removed, and a linen one substituted.

The dreadful preparations completed, the executioner took his station behind the unhappy M—cha—as, and the monk having bestowed his final benediction by sprinkling him with holy water, the cap was pulled over his face, and a double cord passed round his neck and brought to the post. A short stick was introduced through the bights of the cord behind the post, and twisted round. It is doubtful whether brutality or ignorance was the cause of the miserable scene that followed; its horrors baffle description. The cord was twisted so unnecessarily tight, that it broke; a line of blood distinctly showed itself on the white cap where the rope had encircled the neck. The struggles of the agonized victim were dreadful. Another cord was supplied, and the same cruel result again ensued. The wretched M—cha—as succeeded in lifting his cap, and discovered to us a countenance so fraught with reproach, anguish, and unutterable despair, that my soul sickens at the remembrance of his sufferings, nor can his tortured features ever be obliterated from my mind. A general murmur of indignation burst forth from the assembled multitude. I will not harass the feelings of my readers by further details of this distressing scene: suffice it to say that the sufferings of the unhappy M—cha—as were not terminated until the ropes from both his legs were successively applied to effect his strangulation. The body was then taken from the seat, laid at length upon the open platform, and the faggots underneath were ignited. When the flames reached the corpse, the arms extended, and the body turned right round. A smothered cry of horror broke from the majority of the spectators at this extraordinary sight: many believed he was still alive; but by the rational part of the assembly it was supposed to be caused by the action of the heat on the muscles. All that remained of the once gallant young nobleman was quickly reduced to ashes, and were cast into the Tagus, according to the sentence.

> " No farther seek his" errors " to disclose,
> Or draw his frailties from their dread abode."

CHAPTER X.

Convoy a merchant-vessel to Madeira and the Cape de Verd Islands—The Dog and the Turtles—Put into Porto Praya—Slave-ships—Send boats up the Gambia—James's Island—Land-crabs—Horrible resting-place.—Fall in with a Goree trader—Enormous Ant-hills—Flamingoes—Capture a Slave Schooner—Traffic in human flesh—Liberation of Slaves.

Our next trip was to convoy an English merchant-vessel to Madeira and the Cape de Verd Islands. Between the Canaries and the former place we were becalmed for three or four days: during this time we caught a number of turtles sleeping on the surface of the water, sufficient to supply the whole ship's company for a fortnight. Our friend Boatswain proved himself an expert fisher upon this occasion. The first turtle seen created some little bustle abaft, in the anxiety of lowering the stern boat to secure the prize;

Boatswain, hearing the noise, leaped on the taffrail ; his quick eye caught sight of the object we wished to secure, and before we could arrest the descent of the sagacious animal, he had plunged into the deep. The turtle was considered as lost, but the dog, half turning his head in snapping at it, brought his upper jaw upon the under part of the shell of the turtle, and, instantly turning it on its back, rendered his prey powerless. Mr. Boatswain brought the turtle in triumph to the boat that was hastening to meet him : it weighed about twenty-four pounds. I suspect this may be considered a novel feat in the annals of canine sagacity; and probably our favourite stands pre-eminent among his species in performances of this nature. He was truly a nonpareil of a dog, and many of his actions would have done honour to the human race. His extreme anxiety, at sea or in harbour, to seize upon any stray article that might be floating past the ship, amounted almost to a fault ; and once led nearly to the finale of poor Boatswain and the endangering of the lives of a boat's crew —a circumstance which I shall enlarge upon in its proper place.

Off St. Jago we parted with our convoy, and put into Porto Praya Bay to recruit our water and obtain a scanty supply of fresh provisions. During our short stay an English schooner arrived from the coast of Africa: circumstances awakened a suspicion that she was engaged in the illicit traffic of slaves, which being strengthened by a strict search, she was taken possession of and despatched to Sierra Leone for adjudication. This incident altered our destination; instead of immediately returning to Lisbon, we bent our course towards the coast. On the day of our departure we fell in with an American-built ship under Spanish colours, which proving suspicious, we anchored in the roads of the Isle de Mayo in order to search her. The slave-irons, boilers, &c. found among the cargo, determined Captain S—yd to detain her, and she was likewise despatched to Sierra Leone. Another Spaniard, under similar circumstances, was captured the following day.

This succession of luck caused us to run direct for the coast and examine it, on our way down to Freetown. The first place we touched at was the mouth of the Gambia: the boats, well manned and armed, were sent up the river in search of slavers. After entering the river, it expands into a wide stream. The breeze blowing strong against us, we had recourse to our sails to beat to windward, but a sudden serious leak in the pinnace, occasioned by the starting of one of her planks, obliged us all to bear up for the western point that formed the entrance of the river. Here we landed, and found some huts of the natives. Hauling our injured boat on the beach we quickly repaired her. We saw lots of game, including red-legged partridges, but, as sporting was not the object in view, we again departed. Numbers of the natives had assembled to gaze upon us, and, as I was an utter stranger to their character, I thought it wisest to decamp as soon as possible: the significant gestures of the armed part of the spectators boded no good; not that the poor creatures could have effected any thing serious against us, but loss of life is always to be avoided in such cases.—Night had closed in before we reached James's Island, which I had marked out as our first night's resting-place. It is a small spot in the middle of the river, (at this place seven miles broad,) and had formerly been fortified and held by us with a considerable factory. The French took and destroyed the fortifications. It was now unoccupied; the walls alone remained, covered with rank vegetation. We landed our sails, and converted them into tents to protect us from the night air. In exploring the ruins of the castle by torch-light, we found several land-crabs, which the boatswain declared to be excellent eating, particularly as it was impossible they could have fed upon any unwholesome substance. Sailors are impressed with the idea, and with good reason, that these creatures have a particular fancy for the tenants of cemeteries, and they are consequently held in abhorrence by the seamen who have visited the West Indies, where they abound; but when found at distances which ensure them from suspicion of such pollution, they are pronounced excellent food. I never could be persuaded to taste them.

The boatswain, however, who was not extremely nice upon such matters, had made up his mind to have a land-crab supper. Collecting fuel for a fire, he popped upon a board, which, adhering tenaciously to the soil, he with trifling exertion ripped off. His appetite for the crabs took instant flight, on observing that he had got hold of the lid of a coffin. During the night I found my cloak had been spread over one of these receptacles for the dead: the disagreeable discovery was made by the rotten materials giving way and letting me down upon the crumbling skeleton within. I could not sleep after this definition of our resting-place, but walked about till the first grey streak of dawn, with no very pleasant feelings, to while away the time. At daylight we discovered that the place was full of graves. The island itself is a rock, with not sufficient depth of soil to admit of its covering the relics of mortality consigned to its bosom. The upper part of the remaining coffins were all exposed to view.

The fever in this insalubrious climate is fatally destructive to European constitutions, and at that time the loss of life experienced by vessels trading either for slaves or the commodities of the country was always great: their burial-place was James's Island.

We ascended the river, and on the second

day fell in with a Goree small trader, who informed us that we had passed a slaver during the night. The report being confirmed by another vessel of the same description, who stated that nothing was above us, we retraced our way, taking one of the black crew out of the Goree trader as a pilot. Two or three canoes that we had chased ran on shore, and their affrighted crews took shelter in the thickets, abandoning their light barks, and all that they contained, to our mercy: so alarmed were the poor wretches at the idea of being kidnapped. We added to their store, and left a little present in their shallops, in lieu of a monkey we found in one of them; and continued our course downwards.

The banks, as far as we ascended the river, were thickly lined with the mangrove tree, which prevented our landing except here and there. On one of these open spots I went on shore to examine what in the distance appeared to me a haycock. On approaching it, I found it to be a mound raised by the ants. It was at least eight feet high, and I should say from thirty to thirty-five feet in circumference at the base.

How insignificant do the most stupendous works of man appear, when compared with the enormous erections of these tiny industrious insects! I ran my sword into it: and in the breach first appeared the larger class of ant, who came to reconnoitre the cause of this sudden inroad; they disappeared, and quickly returned with myriads of their brethren, the larger class seeming to direct the labours of the smaller. In an incredibly short space of time the breach was repaired. My curiosity would fain have cut out more work for the wonderful powers of these insects, but a rustling and snorting in the thick underwood that surrounded it rather alarmed me, and I retreated to my boat. As we shoved off, I caught a glimpse of the object which had hastened my movements, which was nothing more or less than a buffalo. A musket-shot caused him to back astern, and we saw no more of him.

An open space of mud by the side of the river excited our attention, from the amazing number of flamingoes that covered it. It is somewhere said that these birds may be taken for soldiers at a distance; I can easily believe it, if the military of the country in which they abound, wear red jackets. As we approached the spot where the schooner was said to be lying, I landed, and from a rising ground examined her with my glass: while reconnoitring, I observed a boat full of negroes taken alongside; it was the completion of her cargo.

The crews of our boats were so exhausted with their long tugging at the oar, that I remained some time under cover of the projecting point. We were full five miles off when we left its shelter. They fortunately did not see us till my boat was within a mile of them; the other two had dropped astern above that distance. Observing that they were busily preparing on board for resistance, it was deemed advisable to push on and take our chance, rather than encourage their warlike ideas by any apparent hesitation, or give them the opportunity of running the vessel on shore; we therefore kept steadily on. As we approached her, we hoisted a small English ensign. All hands were evidently well armed for defence; when we got within hail, the commander desired us to keep off, or he would sink us. Without slackening our endeavours to get alongside, the threat was answered by informing him that if he presumed to fire a single shot, we would not leave a soul alive on board. This counter threat had the desired effect; the muzzles of their small-arms were lowered, and I took quiet possession of the vessel, a fine American schooner, Nostra Senhora de los Dolores, under Spanish colours, with a full cargo of slaves, all ready for sailing; she was only awaiting the arrival of the supercargo from the shore. In less than a quarter of an hour he made his appearance,—an American, and the *bona fide* skipper of the craft. Had he been on board, it is probable the capture would not have been made without bloodshed; but, fortunately, the nominal commander, a Spaniard, preferred submission to the risk of an encounter.

As soon as our consorts came alongside, we immediately got under weigh, and made a good stretch down the river before dark, when we anchored for the night.—This traffic in human flesh is most detestable, and, as Englishmen, we cannot but shudder at the wholesale manner in which it was carried on by our own countrymen. What will not the love of lucre effect! it spurs on, and excites the basest passions of mankind. Men who have grown rich in this vilest of all vile pursuits, are even yet to be seen, and they are courted for that polluted wealth which has been drawn from Africa's soil by the cruel abstraction of her children, amidst their cries of anguish and appeals for mercy, drowned in blood and tears!

The sight of one of these pandemoniums afloat is sufficient to rouse all the angry feelings of a man possessed of an iota of humanity, or whose nature has not been completely brutalized by such a course of profligacy. I now descended to the slave-rooms, as they are termed, and witnessed all the worst horrors of slavery. In a space of thirty feet by twenty-five, and scarcely five feet in height, one hundred and fifty unfortunate beings were immured, all in irons. The countenances of some of them displayed deadly hatred and revenge. The supercargo informed me they were desperate dare-devils, and for the safety of the vessel he was obliged to manacle them.

> "The flesh will quiver where the pincers tear,
> The blood will start where the knife is driven."

To his horror, I ordered them to be released;

he begged to be set on shore, as he was confident we should all be murdered. I persisted in my orders, and they were freed from their irons; I endeavoured to make them understand that we had come to release them, but, I fear, without much success. The next was the women's apartment, much smaller in space, and crowded to suffocation—their limbs were unfettered, but liberty of movement there was none; many of the younger ones were without clothing of any description, and the others had merely a cloth round their waists. The after-room contained the children from five years of age to ten or eleven, attended by some of the elder women. Altogether, it was a sickening scene, a damning evidence of European (more properly, in this instance, American) depravity. I felt relieved as I again inhaled the sweet breath of heaven.

CHAPTER XI.

Remarks on the Slave Question.

HERE, perhaps, it may not be amiss to glance across the Atlantic. But before I touch upon that momentous subject, involving the question of West India slavery, and the present condition of Negroes in the Colonies, let it be fully understood that I am in no way personally interested or connected with that description of property; that no man can more heartily detest the traffic in human flesh than myself; and that I fully admit (what cannot be denied by the most specious sophistry,) that, according to the natural rights of man, one man cannot enslave another.

Nevertheless, from the remotest ages into which the mind of man can penetrate, slavery has been permitted to exist. Among the chosen people of God, bondage assumed its mildest form, and the bondmen and bondwomen were treated as part of the family of the patriarchs. Abraham speaks of his steward, born in his house, being his heir, in case of failure of issue. Yet these men were saleable, and transferrable from one master to another, like flocks and herds. If slavery is one of those evils that has for some purpose of infinite wisdom been permitted for ages to prevail, there appears but one mode of redeeming the stain supposed to be attached to civilized nations on that account. It is the formation of such laws as shall ensure the protection and well-being of the Negro: laws that will lead to the gradual enfranchisement of his mind from the slough of demoralization that at present surrounds it, without violently snapping the bonds that bind him to his master, until he can govern his actions from moral impulses.

I set out with boldly averring, that the well-behaved Negro in the Colonies would not exchange his slavery and his comfort for English freedom and a precarious subsistence. It is a morbid sensibility that would invest men scarcely emerged from barbarism, with feelings that can only belong to beings possessed of the highest order of mental and moral intellect. But before I proceed with my own observations on this point, I think it will not be uninteresting to a large portion of my readers to give a short sketch of the rise and progress of slavery.

It has never been doubted that slavery had its origin in war: sovereigns, in their contests with each other, either massacred their prisoners in cold blood, or condemned them to perpetual slavery. But we have no means of proving that slavery commenced with savages. The traffic in men prevailed almost universally long before the Roman name or Latin language was heard of; and we are, moreover, led to infer, from the curse denounced by Noah upon Ham and Canaan after the deluge, that slavery existed before that event.

"Nimrod, the son of Cush the son of Ham, was a mighty hunter before the Lord." Whatever might have been his superiority in the chase over his contemporaries, we can scarcely suppose it earned for him this appellation, it being the chief occupation of men at that dark period; and it is with more justice believed he was a mighty hunter of men. His inheritance was small, and Scripture tells us he increased it by violence and conquest, seized upon Babylon, founded the kingdom of Assyria, and became the first monarch; he made bondmen of the captives taken in his wars, and compelled them to work; and therefore from this epoch we date post-diluvian slavery.

The Bible is sufficient evidence that the practice of buying and selling servants existed in the time of the Patriarchs, and descended to their posterity; it formed the most valuable portion of their wealth. This traffic was fully authorized by the Jewish law. But great as was the power invested in the Hebrews over their heathen bondmen, yet they were expressly prohibited from acquiring this species of property by any other means than that of lawful purchase. " He that stealeth a man," saith Moses, " and selleth him, shall surely be put to death."

By degrees slavery lost the mild form appertaining to it under the chosen people of God, and it became an abomination among the Pagan nations of antiquity in the East, and slowly, but too surely found its way into every country on the face of the earth. In the time of the Greeks and Romans, all prisoners, whatever might be their sex, rank, and station, were liable to become slaves, and subjected to the vilest drudgery and most cruel treatment.

The Thebans were sold as slaves by Philip of Macedon after the conquest of that kingdom. In Sparta the slaves were treated with the utmost cruelty, although upon their industry and exertions depended the subsistence of their brutal masters. The Spartan youth were moreover allowed to show their dexterity in butchering the unhappy slaves, and it is related that on one occasion three thousand perished in this manner. Of the cruelty of the Romans to their slaves history affords too many striking proofs: prisoners of war were all slaves. Camillus sold his Etrurian captives. Fabius reduced thirty thousand citizens of Tarentum to slavery, and sold them like cattle to the highest bidder. Julius Cæsar sold at one time fifty-three thousand captives for slaves: this great general has never been taxed with wanton cruelty, nevertheless he made slaves of his fellow men : the foulest blot that rests upon his memory is justly considered to be his conduct towards the noble, generous, and chivalrous Vercingetorix. This truly great man had long skilfully and successfully baffled the best-concocted schemes of the Roman general. To save his wretched country from further misery, he voluntarily offered himself as a sacrifice to appease the wrath of Cæsar. It was accepted. But Vercingetorix was too great to be pardoned ; he was loaded with irons, chained to the triumphal car of the conqueror, and after many years of cruel suffering finally immolated.

Captives were not the only slaves in Rome ; debtors might be seized by their creditors, and compelled to labour in their service until the debt was discharged. A noble Roman who died some years before Christ, left to his heirs upwards of four thousand slaves.

The slaves in Rome were frequently branded on the forehead when suspected of intended evasion. The introduction of Christianity in some degree ameliorated the sad condition of the slaves, even under heathen masters ; but slavery continued to exist in the empire and its dependencies for many ages after the conversion of the Emperor Constantine.

In ancient Germany the slaves were attached to the soil, employed generally for the purposes of agriculture, and seldom imprisoned, beaten, or enchained: they were not considered as articles of traffic, except those who had been originally freemen, and had lost their freedom by gambling.

We now touch upon British soil. It appears by a statute of Alfred the Great, that the purchase of a man without a voucher to guarantee the sale was distinctly prohibited. In that statute the lords of the creation are classed with oxen and horses. It is presumed the law was enacted to prevent the abduction of men; but it is a detestable proof, that, so late as the ninth or tenth century, an Englishman, when fairly bought, was as truly the property of the purchaser as his horse, his ox, or his ass.

We also learn that bondmen and bondwomen existed in the reign of Elizabeth; and that in the year 1574 a commission of inquiry was issued respecting their property, and their emancipation compounded for, so " that they might enjoy their lands and goods as freemen." *

It is little known that, in Scotland, colliers and salters were slaves till within the last sixty years, when an act passed the British legislature for their manumission and restoration to the rights of freemen. Until that period the sons of these men were obliged to follow the employment of their fathers: they were attached by birth to certain mines, and their services could only be transferred to other proprietors by the consent of the lord of the manor to whose soil the mine belonged.

History informs us that slavery has always existed in Africa in its most terrible form, beginning with the atrocities committed in Carthage, and tracing it through the different states of that partially explored country. From the only means afforded us of investigating this subject, it appears a matter of doubt whether the poor negro, at any period however remote, was absolutely secure of his personal freedom. It is a great mistake to

* Kames's Sketches.

suppose that negro slavery originated with the Portuguese; I think it is Gibbon who proves that an extensive traffic in woolly-headed negroes had been carried on some centuries before the Portuguese were aware of there being such a place as the coast of Guinea. The negroes have, in all probability, been slaves to the Arabs for ages, and that slavery has continued uninterrupted among this people since the time of their great ancestor Ishmael. It is also evident that negroes were exposed for sale in foreign countries so early as the sixth century, and that they were then greatly prized in Egypt and Arabia. From the observations made by European travellers, we are led to suspect that slavery has existed from time immemorial among the negroes themselves, enslaving each other without compunction as opportunity presented itself.

It is proved by authors who are neither blinded by prejudice nor enthusiasm, and who hold the abominable traffic in utter detestation, that slavery of the most revolting kind must have existed among the negro tribes long before the Arabs and Portuguese entered upon this traffic, although these nations may have been the first to transplant them from their native soil.

I have given a short sketch from the best authorities of the rise and progress of slavery, and having arrived at that point which relates to the fact of negro bondage (as proved beyond a doubt) having prevailed in their own country; it now becomes a matter of serious import and deep interest to examine into the state of West India slavery, and to determine whether, since the abolition of the slave trade, the negro's condition in the West Indies is not at this moment infinitely better and happier than it would have been in his own country. In short, the traffic of negroes has only been transferred from the Arabs of Barbary to European Christian nations. That men bearing that sacred name should have embarked in so unholy a pursuit, is a disgrace that can only be blotted from the national records by the contrition of their descendants, and wise enactments for the negro's comfort and final entry into the bosom of an enlightened Church.

Let us take a review of the treatment of the blacks under the old French regime. It is such as conveys a well-merited reproach to the British legislature of that period. In the French colonies the slaves " who cultivated the plantations, were attached to the soil, and could not be drawn off to pay debts, or be sold separately from the estate on which they lived. This gave them a lasting property in their huts and little spots of ground, which they might safely cultivate without dread of being turned out of possession, or transferred, contrary to their interests and feelings, from one proprietor to another. They were under the protection of law as soon as they arrived in the colony. Proper missionaries were appointed for the purpose of training them up to a certain degree of religious knowledge, and ample funds were allotted for the maintenance of those ecclesiastics.

" On ill treatment received from his master, or on being deprived of his allowance of food and raiment, the slave was directed to apply to the king's attorney, who was obliged to prosecute the master forthwith. That officer was also bound to prosecute, if by any other means he heard of the abuse; the law adding as the reason, *This we will to be observed to check the abuse of power in the master."* *

Had such wise and beneficial regulations been adopted in our own colonies, Great Britain would not have had to blush for the misdeeds and cruelties of some of her sons, or to mourn, as she probably will ere twenty years are over our heads, the loss of those valuable possessions, the great nursery of our seamen, and the ruin of thousands of calumniated men, many of whom have already sunk into an untimely grave, overwhelmed with despair at the accusations brought against them, and at the present and future prospects of their families. What can we say for the liberality of men who mercilessly asperse the character of the present well-educated and humane body of gentlemen planters, and would punish in their persons the crimes of past ages, and the errors of former English governments?

If colonial slavery be a crime, it is a crime that was not only sanctioned, but insisted upon by the British government, and the possession of a definite number of negroes formed the *sine qua*

---

* Ramsay's Essay on the Treatment and Miseries of Slaves.

non for granting a certain tract of land to settlers, who, in the full confidence of British faith, embarked their whole fortune in the adventure.

The slave-trade has been abolished by the enlightened nations of England and France, and with it has ceased the misery consequent upon the ready supply to any demand that might be made; but, in defiance of the treaties and conventions made by the former power with other countries, there is proof positive that an extensive traffic in slaves is still carried on in Cuba and the Brazils.

In the year 1826, when I was stationed at Jamaica, a slave-vessel, with four hundred negroes from the coast of Africa, under French colours, nominally bound to Martinique, was brought into Port Royal by one of our cruisers;[*] but from our treaty with that nation, Vice-Admiral Sir Laurence Halsted, notwithstanding this palpable falsehood, was obliged to release her immediately, and it was supposed she landed her cargo on the island of Cuba.

[*] Between nine hundred and a thousand miles to leeward of her declared destination.

Unless all the nations of Christendom are agreed upon its extermination, the native Africans are in no way benefited by this law. It has been prosecuted in all ages and under all religions, and, until nature herself shall change, we must fear it ever will be so. And supposing the abominable traffic among Christian nations should entirely cease, it will then revert to the former, and original, dealers in negro slaves. If slavery is to exist, it may be so modified and softened as to leave nothing but the odious word 'slave' to be regretted in the compact between master and negro; and if we examine minutely into the real state of the case, we cannot divest ourselves of the belief, that the negroes may be much happier in the West Indies under mild regulations, paternal care, and practical religious instruction, than the most liberal stretch of visionary philanthropy can figure them to be, in a savage state in their native land, enslaved by each other, the prey to bloodthirsty men and contending factions. We cannot blind ourselves to the fact, that the actual state of barbarism pervading every part of Africa precludes any reasonable hope of the negroes witnessing the benefit of a moral and religious existence.

"Out of evil springeth good:" no well-disposed person can seriously deny that slavery is an evil; yet by proper management, thousands of human beings may eventually be made to feel that they are responsible for their actions, and equally enjoy the blessings bestowed on black and white men, instead of dragging out a miserable existence in Africa, but little removed in mind or feeling from the brute creation. That negroes are happy in our West India colonies I have had ocular demonstration; and that they understand not the word freedom in the sense we wish them to understand it, is not less morally certain. To set them free in their present state of ignorance and cunning, is as wild and Utopian a project as ever entered the heads of reasonable beings, and can only have been agitated by men totally unacquainted with their nature, customs, and habits. The negroes will not thank the English legislature for the species of freedom intended to be given them;—they must eat, drink, and be clothed at another's expense, do no work, and live in a constant state of idleness and libertinism; and this is the *summum bonum* of their idea of happiness and freedom.

I have studied much the general character of the children of the African torrid zone. My profession has brought me repeatedly in contact with them, in Africa, the West Indies, and America. I have had free negro servants who had been emancipated in their first childhood, and who (according to the generally received opinion that the negro's vices are co-existent with slavery) ought to have been uncontaminated by the negro leaven. But such was not the case; they were negroes in every sense of the word —intolerable thieves, and so impudent therewithal that it required the utmost stock of patience and philosophy to restrain myself from bringing them to summary chastisement. Even the Mandingo boy who was attached to my person at six years of age, and whom I had caused to be christened and educated, was such an incorrigible thief that I was finally obliged to dismiss him; and it was high time, for I was nearly minus my wardrobe. Perhaps the good people of England consider theft upon the part of negroes a very venial crime: with a newly imported negro it might have been the case, but they were soon made to understand the import of theft, and its consequent punishment. They are neither transported, nor hung, for a breach of the eighth commandment; that is a privilege only belonging to a free people.

In 1825 I was stationed off the north-west coast of Ireland: it would be in vain for me to depict the true state of abject misery and poverty of the unhappy people in that district; willingly would I have shut my eyes to the sight, and closed my ears to the sound of such degradation and wretchedness existing in any spot of the British dominions. I gladly quitted the land of freedom and human misery for the West India colonies: the contrast was striking, but it admitted of the grateful conviction that slavery existed but in name, and that it was totally free from all those horrors and abominations which the fertile imaginations of our fire-side philanthropists are pleased to lay at the door of West India proprietors, or their managers. It is possible that, among so large a body of men, instances of oppression and cruelty may occasionally be found; but let us look at home, and we shall not have far to seek for more flagrant offences than can with justice be laid to their account. Compare the condition of the labouring negro with the same class of men in England and Ireland. The negro is well fed, sufficiently clothed, possesses a well-constructed hut, furnished in accordance with the negro's ideas of comfort; he reposes upon a good bed, he has a garden well stocked with vegetables and fruit, the seeds and plants supplied by his master; he has pigs, poultry, and a certain quantity of provision-ground, from the produce of which the industrious negro may lay by, upon an average, from fifteen to twenty pounds a year. In sickness he is nursed and supplied with medical attendance and drugs at his master's expense. The children of field-negroes are taken care of in the estate nursery, and allowances allotted to them from their birth. But to counterbalance all these blessings he is a slave; that is, he is compelled to work against his free will, (and who is there that can always follow the dictates of his own free will ?) for the benefit of his master, from whom he has received the above enumerated comforts, five or six days in the week, from half-past six in the morning till five in the evening, of which time a couple of hours are consumed at his meals. The women, before their confinements, are exempted from work, attended at the crisis with assiduous care, and provided with nurses. The labours of the day ended, mirth and jollity reign among the sable race ; the lively dance delights the eye of the stranger, the jocund laugh sounds sweetly on his ear. He asks himself, Is this slavery ? Is this the state of things we wish to see annihilated ? Are these fine estates to be destroyed, these happy people to be plunged into discontent, anarchy, and bloodshed, because the ignorant clamour of nine hundred and ninety-nine out of a thousand will it so ? It is indeed one of the misfortunes attendant on the free press of our free country, that well-meaning people are unresistingly carried away by the impetus of popular declamation. The flood-gates of mischief have been opened; may the torrent be arrested in its course before it inundates the plain !

But to return to my negro: he lies down upon his bed, unoppressed with care for the morrow; no visions of poverty rack his peace of mind; he knows that in sickness or health, in youth or age, he is equally the object of care. His quarrels, hopes, and fears, are alike submitted to the adjudication, sympathy, or condolence of his master.

It has always appeared to me, that the principal hardship arising out of the position of the negro, is comprised in the separation of families, and the dissolution of the ties of consanguinity and affection;—it is imagined that such misery would attend the removal of members of a family to distant estates. In some few instances this circumstance might be felt, but, in far the greater part of the negro population, these ties are either not cherished, or so fragile in their nature as to render it a matter of no serious moment to the persons concerned. Negro mothers are, in general, most outrageous in their conduct towards their offspring, and indeed occasionally their savage conduct towards each other is sufficiently indicative of a spirit which proves that they are bound by no moral ties or government of the passions.

The domestic negroes enjoy an enviable position, and look down with pity and contempt upon the drudgery of an English servant. Now, let any Englishman ask himself, Is this the situation of the labouring poor, or of the manufacturing classes of this country? Of the state of the peasantry of some parts of Ireland it is painful to speak. I have traversed the world north and south, east and west, and never yet have I beheld an equal extent of wretchedness;—but the Irish are free—free to transport their poverty and their misery to any country to which they choose to drag their squalid bodies and weary limbs. When the substantial attributes of freedom are confounded and obscured by the mist of ignorance, its shadow becomes unduly worshipped, and artful and designing men gain a dangerous ascendancy over minds incompetent to grapple with the loftier virtues, or to appreciate the patriotic qualities upon which the basis of a just and generous sense of freedom is founded. Emancipated negroes are, generally speaking, the most idle and impudent beings in existence. I once requested a negro to assist one of my boat's crew in lifting a package upon his shoulders. The fellow looked at me with the contemptuous smile of an Eastern Bashaw, and screamed into my ear, "Good Goramity, wha' you tak me for Coast ob Guinea nigger?" He had purchased his freedom only the day before.

My observations on the negro character lead me to fear that the cultivation of the cane by negro free labour will be found next to hopeless. The kingdom of Hayti offers a warning example on this head. Is there any visible sign that the negroes of our colonies are farther advanced in civilization than the Haytians, who have been in possession for the last thirty years of the much-prized, but scarcely defined boon, freedom? Under the French, St. Domingo supplied France beyond the demand with sugar; now it barely raises more than sufficient for its own consumption. We cannot so deceive ourselves.

The last time I was stationed in the West Indies, I was on a visit to a gentleman in the interior of Jamaica; and a stout-looking negro stood behind his chair at dinner. Sambo quitted the room, when his master observed, "There is a fellow to whom I have repeatedly offered freedom, but he has always rejected it."

The following morning, in a solitary ramble before breakfast, I encountered Mr. Sambo.

"Good morning, Sambo!"

"Good marning, Massa!"

"Well, Sambo, is it true that you do not want to become a free man?"

"Yees, Massa,—wha' for me hab my freedom?—pose um free, massa no gie me for yam—pose um sick, um no hab doctor—Sambo grow old, um no can wurruk, what can poor Sambo do?"

"But you are rich, Sambo; your master tells me you have money enough to purchase your freedom three times over."

"But, Massa, pose um free — um pend too much ebery day—Den Massa, you sabbe, me like gie someting to my piccaninny when Sambo go to Pompy parlour."*

"But, when you are free, you can work for yourself, and get more money."

"No, dank you—Massa, um good massa, Sambo like um bery much,—No wish for free."

* The grave.

And away went Mr. Sambo, grinning with pleasure at what he doubtless conceived unanswerable arguments in favour of his determination.

Such I have ever found the predominant feeling among the better class of house negroes. Although the gains of the negro are, strictly speaking, the property of the master, the owner who would assume such a right would be scouted from society. I never heard of a solitary instance of a planter taking advantage of this power; on the contrary, the property of a negro (not unfrequently amounting to two or three hundred pounds) is rigidly distributed among his relations and friends according to his last wishes.

Oftentimes have I been surprised at seeing little jetty woolly-headed beings crawl from under the table-cloth to get a nice tit-bit from massa or misses, and again hide themselves until it was time for more. It may be argued that self-interest is the main spring of action in the care taken of the negro: it may have its weight, but it can never prompt the many kindnesses and attentions bestowed upon them, not at all necessary to the existence, or conducive to the health of the negro. But, supposing that self-interest is the *primum mobile* of the planters' actions, where do we find any deficiency of that quality in the various relations of social life? It appears to me to be the governing principle of every condition of people, from the peasant to the monarch; and why should an undue share of it be lodged upon the shoulders of the colonists?

Whatever may be the present state of the negro, yet, as the most refined nations of the earth were once hordes of barbarians, there is no reason to justify the belief that in process of time the negro may not become as other men. We are therefore pursuing the path of duty, by cautiously endeavouring to advance that end; whether such a result will be a future benefit to this country is a matter not difficult of solution.

It is not to be supposed that, if the negroes *ever* arrive at a point of intellectual equality with white men, they will be governed by others than themselves: consequently, the white population will no longer hold a paramount footing in the West Indies. At present they acknowledge our superiority; they prefer being the slaves of a white master, to serving one of their own colour.

However much I should wish to have the contrary proved, I cannot cheat myself into the belief that the negro is in point of mental capacity equal to a white man, although he may possess qualities well worthy of cultivation and improvement.

The vices said to be most conspicuous among this unhappy race on their native soil are, " idleness, treachery, revenge, cruelty, impudence, stealing, lying, and debauchery." The principles of natural law are smothered, and the reproof of conscience silenced. Every person acquainted with the negro character has found it to possess more or less of these vices; and when the state of society in Africa is duly considered, we cannot be surprised that negroes are revengeful, treacherous, and cruel. Even in civilized countries, gifted with science, religion, and a code of enlightened laws, all these vices individually exist. We must therefore feel some degree of compassion for our sable brethren, three-fourths of whom in their native land are slaves to the rest, and whose offspring are born to no other inheritance.

" Most parts of the coast differ in their governments; some are absolute monarchies, whilst others draw near to an aristocracy. In both, the authority of the chief or chiefs is unlimited, extending to life, and is exercised as often as criminal cases require, unless death is commuted to slavery, in which case the offender is sold, and, if the shipping will not buy the criminal, he is immediately put to death. Fathers of free condition have power to sell their children, but this power is seldom enforced." *

The Congo negroes will sell their children for articles however trifling.† Polygamy to any extent is permitted; wives may be repudiated or sold, and husbands and concubines are got rid of, at mutual will and pleasure. Obi, or witchcraft, in which all negroes firmly believe, is also punished with slavery: debtors and their families incur the same penalty; and it is feared that, if there were no buyers, the poor wretches would be murdered.

" To those persons who fancy that the wars

* Edwards's History of the West Indies, vol. ii.
† Modern Universal History, vol. xiii.

between the African princes are carried on for the sole purpose of supplying the European ships with slaves, it may be proper to remark that one of the kings of Dahomy slaughtered at once not only all the captives taken in war, but also one hundred and twenty-seven prisoners of different kinds, that he might have a sufficiency of skulls to adorn the walls of his palace; though at the very time of that massacre he *knew* that there were six slave-ships in the road of Whidah, from which he could have got for every prime slave a price little short of thirty pounds sterling." *

"The King of Dahomy's dwelling occupies a space of about a mile square. It consists of a multitude of huts formed of mud walls with bamboo roofs: and the whole is enclosed by a mud wall twenty feet in height. The entrance of the king's apartment is paved with human skulls, and the side walls are ornamented with the jaw-bones of men. On the thatched roofs numerous human skulls are ranged on wooden stakes, and he declares war by announcing that his house wants thatch."

* Dalzell's History of the Kingdom of Dahomy.

In short, the great mass of the negro population are viewed as the property of chiefs, and sold as such. Now, with these facts before us, what have we to deplore in the actual position of the West India negro? The negroes' corporeal condition no longer requires the pity of the English people, much less their tears and sighs;—these, and their holy exertions, may with more propriety and justice be reserved for the benefit of a large portion of their own countrymen —for the suffering peasantry of Ireland—for the unhappy overworked children of the manufactories. When the refulgent light of Christianity, and the mild precepts of our Saviour shall have worked their way into the negro's heart, then may we hope that the proper time for emancipation is arrived; but other hands than those of the mistaken men to whom their conversion has been erroneously entrusted, must be employed, if any hope of ultimate success be entertained.

Is it the word slave alone that is to excite our sympathy? or do we envy their superiority of condition over the poor of Great Britain and Ireland, a melancholy part of whom beg, rob, and plunder for a subsistence?

Why should we make the negro discontented with his lot? The native Africans bless their present state of bondage, when compared with what they suffered in their own torrid zone. If the happiness of the negro is really the object that occupies the mind of the people of this country, the West Indies is not the spot upon which they should exercise their calling. They must penetrate the wilds of Africa; build churches and towns; appoint ministers and responsible officers; establish manufactures; and frame laws suitable to the character of the nation to be civilized.

Prominent differences are to be found among the several negro tribes. The Koromantyns are ferocious and stubborn, but well adapted to work, firm in body and mind, and in no way deficient in courage. The Eboes are constitutionally timid, and sometimes melancholy. The Mandingoes are considered gentle in their dispositions, but are more addicted to the vice of theft than the rest of the African tribes. The Whydah, or Paupaws as they are called in the West Indies, are considered to be the best-dispositioned slaves; but they are great thieves, apprehensive of death, and given to gaming. "The softer virtues are seldom found in the bosom of the enslaved African; give him sufficient authority, and he becomes the most remorseless of tyrants." *

Their cruelty to the brute creation exceeds all belief; cutting, maiming, and poisoning animals are of frequent occurrence, and form the chief grounds for corporal punishment in the West Indies. Even the faithful dog, the companion of man, meets with no kind usage from a negro master.

These are the materials upon which the philanthropist has to work. The labour would be Herculean, but such as befits the Christian-like spirit that engrosses the restless and active minds of Englishmen; and if it be the will of an omniscient Deity, that after countless ages of darkness, iniquity, and suffering, a free and happy black population shall exist beneath the influence of a torrid zone, then indeed may our posterity in future ages look back upon the deeds of their ancestors with veneration and admiration. At present it amounts almost to presumption to believe, that, with a few strokes of the pen, man can

* Edwards's History of the West Indies.

annihilate the inscrutable and mysterious purposes of the Creator, change the nature of the negro, and invest him at once with that moral and intellectual superiority which can alone place him on a level with his more fortunate white brethren.

Of itself the word slavery speaks volumes of offence to an English ear. There is, however, much in a name. We will endeavour to define the obnoxious word, and separate it from the thousand and one feelings that may be supposed to give weight and colour to the whole: this done, we may be somewhat startled, perhaps displeased, to find (as regards the West India question) a skeleton remaining in the place of the apparently intangible mass of matter which, in all the consciousness of security, we submitted to the process of a fearless decomposition. It is averred that slavery is a word generally understood, but its proper definition difficult.

I have asserted that there is much in a name, and I think my premiss will not be falsified. The word slave, in its original sense, was synonymous with *noble and illustrious*; but these noble and illustrious people having been sold by the Romans, on the decline of the Roman empire, to the Venetians, they were thence dispersed all over Europe, and hence the term slave became a byword, as denoting the state of servitude of a class of men who were considered the absolute property of their master. The Roman orator thus defines slavery — " Servitus est obedientia fracti animi et abjecti, et arbitrio carentis suo,"—" whether the unhappy person fell into that state with or without his own consent or contract." One of our best moral writers states it to be " an obligation to labour for the benefit of the master without the consent or contract of the servant." In modern times there appears but one meaning attached to the word slave, namely, that it can only be applied to men who are bought and sold like beasts. May not the term, however, with much more propriety be applied to the man who deprives himself of his freedom in discharge of a debt which he has voluntarily contracted, and which he is otherwise unable to cancel ? Where does there exist a more degrading species of slavery than that which envelopes the determined gamester? he jeopardises his liberty by his own contract. " It cannot be denied that they who lose their freedom are slaves." Spendthrifts, debtors, the perpetrators of crime, come therefore under this denomination, though the period of their slavery must depend upon circumstances, such as the satisfaction of the creditor, or the nature of the crime to be atoned for. If we search diligently into the origin of our actions, if we examine the motives that govern us, and unravel the complicated state of society and its insufferable exactions, we shall find our strongest inclinations thwarted, our freedom of will fettered, our speech restricted, our movements regulated, our spirits subdued, our enjoyments marred, by that tyrannical bugbear, the world's opinion, and its spurious offspring fashion.

Upon what ground the English nation, above all others, piques itself upon its happy exemption from slavery, is at least equivocal. True, we receive no stripes, our limbs are unshackled, we may go where we list, (save and except where fashion exerts her arbitrary sway ; there is no reservation as to her despotic behests; our dearest interests are laid prostrate at her shrine); but there is a state of mental servitude, a slavish prostration of mind to wealth and exterior appearance, to be found among the higher circles of this country, which might be suffered to sink into the contempt it merits, were it not that the pernicious example silently works its way, with melancholy results, into the more sober part of the community, thence descending into every grade of society conceiving themselves entitled to that misused word gentility, or respectability.

The slavery of the mind and feelings is more galling than that of the body: the vexed spirit will at times rise superior to human manacles, and assert its ascendancy; but its struggles are as a passing meteor in the sky, to dazzle, astonish, and confound,—they ever terminate in defeat. We are enchained, body and mind, hand and foot, by the monster of our own creation.

I have far outrun the limits I had prescribed to myself on a question which has so universally engrossed the minds of my countrymen; indeed I should not have approached the subject of negro slavery, did I not consider the West India question as involving that of the permanent glory of our country.

It would argue a culpable apathy on the part of the members of the naval profession towards the best interests of the nation, did they not keenly watch and examine into proceedings bearing a *prima facie* case of evil to the continued supremacy of the British navy over that element upon which it has so long triumphantly displayed its power.

How far the commercial interest may be affected by a change of system in the colonies, it is not my purpose to agitate. It must be obvious to every man, that the naval and commercial interests of this country are inextricably blended together; depress the one, and the other is immediately affected by it. Destroy our trade with the West Indies and our North American colonies, and the power of the navy is rent to its base. The commerce of England owes its security to the navy :—the navy draws its vital breath from the commercial marine. It is from the extensive trade with our colonies in the western hemisphere that we draw our most experienced seamen, who from boyhood have been accustomed to the vicissitudes of climate and weather. Every West India trader is by law obliged to take a certain number of apprentices, according to the tonnage of the vessel; thus keeping up a constant supply of ablebodied seamen. The trade between the mother country, the West India, and North American colonies, employs British shipping to the amount of eight hundred thousand tons and forty thousand British seamen.* The inference, surely, is plain to the most obtuse understanding, that, if by any legislative enactment we destroy this source of national strength, it must strike the severest blow that has ever fallen upon these realms.

A seaman cannot, like a recruit, be formed in six months; it requires more than that number of years to form a tolerably good sailor. It is a profession embracing such a variety of incidental and novel circumstances, that unexpected knowledge may at all times be drawn from events by the oldest and most experienced seaman.

Our rivals must inwardly congratulate themselves on the wanton act that would lop off the

* See a well-written article on the West India question, as connected with our naval supremacy, in the United Service Journal for July 1833.

finest branches of the parent oak, and doubtless view the wound thus inflicted with greedy satisfaction, in the hope that it will prove the commencement of a decay that may finally eat into the heart of the noble tree, and lay it low before the first blast of scarcely concealed hate and open enmity.

It is to be hoped that a sympathy founded on unjust premises and false conclusions may have but an ephemeral existence, and that men will awake from the trance of mental inanition, to which, at the bidding of fanatics and mistaken zealots, they have passively yielded themselves. The slavery question may truly be regarded as a species of epidemic. People labouring under the malady discard truth and reflection, and swallow with all the avidity of disease the nauseous draughts so dexterously administered as at once to feed and keep up a perpetual irritation of the mind. Englishmen unhappily possess an irresistible desire to force upon other people their own ideas of happiness: it matters not whether there exist a diversity of climate, habits, religion, tastes, capacity, constitution, laws, &c.; we robe the judgment and feelings of others with our own cherished standard of civil, political, moral, and religious excellence, and are unwilling to allow the possibility of happiness existing in any country, or among any people, situated and governed differently to ourselves.

In what does the sum of human happiness consist? It is a question not easily answered; for it is evident that circumstances which produce the greatest store of happiness to one set of men, are incapable of exciting the same feeling in another. The word happy is a relative term, and must be comparatively used. It may be suspected that power, birth, wealth, rank, and other adventitious etceteras, constitute this desirable possession; but happiness is not based upon a superiority of condition; if it were, what a melancholy preponderance of wretchedness would be found in the world!

It is not my intention to dilate upon the many sources whence happiness or misery are derived; it appears tolerably conclusive, that the former is a gift pretty equally distributed among the different orders of society, and that a beneficent Creator has largely compensated both men and animals for those deficiencies which we in our finite conceptions vain-gloriously style the accessories of a happy state of being. The happiness of the negro is the ostensible motive of action: people, excited by the *ignis fatuus* of universal liberty, madly rush to the conclusion, without stopping to deliberate upon the existence of a variety of causes that may prove insufficient and even inimical to the happiness of beings divided from us by gigantic barriers.

Hence a vast majority of the unreflecting portion of the community have decided, that a negro cannot be happy unless he be corporeally free, although he exchange for that freedom a positive amount of blessings, the possession of which is allowed to produce a certain quantity of happiness to every human being.

The present state of West India slavery presents a vast field for fair and open discussion. Let the people be disabused of their errors; let them be made to understand that the negro neither values nor desires the species of liberty we would confer upon him; let Englishmen maturely reflect upon the indissoluble connection existing between a prosperous West India trade and the natural bulwark of this country; and that the destruction of the one will ensure the downfall of the other. If the minds of my countrymen be permitted to acquire a healthier tone, they will feel that they are not called upon, either by the principles of justice, religion, or charity, to immolate themselves upon the altar of philanthropic feeling or sensibility. In their anxiety to burst the bonds of the negro, let them beware of forging the first links of the chain that shall bind their country, and their posterity, to the triumphal car of some future Continental despot.

> "England never did, nor ever shall
> Lie at the proud foot of the conqueror,
> But when it first did help to wound itself."

CHAPTER XII.

Rejoin the Myrtle—Precautions to preserve the health of the Ship's Company—March of a body of White Ants—They are molested—Their revenge—Descendants of the Maroons—" General Montague"—Fruit at Sierra Leone—A Slave-brig —Tragical Occurrence—A White Negress—A captive boy taken as a Servant—His incorrigible propensity to theft— Parrots—Polly and Blacky—Ordered to the assistance of the Arethusa—Tornadoes—An Accident—A second trip up the Gambia—A Black Trafficker in Slaves—Bivouac on James's Island—Deleterious atmosphere of the Gambia— Arrive at Goree—A Native shipped as a Landsman— Anecdote.

To return to the captured schooner.—The excited fears of the Supercargo proved groundless; the poor wretches, freed from their shackles, stretched their benumbed limbs, and, extending themselves on the deck, slept quietly and soundly; nor was any movement observed among them warranting the suspicion of their intention to rise upon their liberators.

On the approach of dawn we were again under weigh; and before sunset we rejoined the Myrtle. The following day we left the mouth of the Gambia, and, in company with the Slaver, made the best of our way to Sierra Leone. Arrived off the entrance to that river, we fell in with the three other detained vessels, and sailing into the port together, anchored off Freetown. We found the Tigress gun-brig here, the lieutenant commanding her being governor *pro tempore*. It is a beautiful anchorage, and the new colony appeared well laid out: the mountains in the background (whence the place derives its name) add to the beauty of the prospect. The heat is intolerable before the sea breeze sets in about noon. Unfortunately we arrived at the commencement of the rainy season. Every precaution was adopted to preserve the health of the ship's company: the hanging stoves were suspended in the between-decks every morning after the latter were cleaned; the strictest attention was paid to keeping the interior of the vessel as free from damp as possible; the danger arising from noxious air engendered by moisture in a confined space was thus avoided. The crew were never exposed to the sun or rain, Koroo men being always employed in the boats. Though we were detained here a long time waiting for the decision of the Admiralty Court respecting the captured vessels, and afterwards by the Arethusa striking on a rock at the Isle de Los, our cases of fever were very few, and in no instance proved mortal. The rains came down in torrents from the mountains, and the intense heat of the sun, which occasionally broke out at intervals between the heavy showers, was dreadfully oppressive. The awnings were constantly kept sloped; notwithstanding our daily morning scrubbings, the drippings from them turned the water-ways quite green.

Our visits to the shore were few, but, when we did land, there was no lack of attention and hospitality on the part of the upper mercantile ranks; horses were always at our command, and I enjoyed many a gallop, when the weather would permit of our taking that exercise. In one of these excursions my attention was drawn to the line of march of a body of those destructive insects the white ants. They extended farther than I could trace them; their route was directed across the road we were riding, parallel with which flowed a small rill of water. The great body kept in a close line, and were apparently under the command of ants at least twelve times larger than the general mass, who marched on either side. It was a curious and most interesting sight to witness the manner in which they effected a passage over the rill of water; hundreds of thousands of them voluntarily sacrificed themselves for the public weal, by forming with their bodies a bridge, which enabled millions, nay billions of these insects, to pass over. I dismounted, and was left to my own observations by my companions, who were tired out with waiting for me; I was absorbed in contemplation of the manœuvres of this innumerable host of tiny creatures. It would have been well for me had I confined myself to mere observation, but the demon of mischief prompted me to place my foot directly across their path, and endeavour to turn them. I paid dearly for my utter ignorance of their powers of revenge; my leg was instantly covered with them, but my boots prevented me from immediately feeling the effects of their anger. The upper part of the leather scaled, then indeed I became fully sensible of my folly; I was *sans caleçon*, and these little atoms dug their forceps into my flesh, creating intolerable pain. I danced about like one demented, beating the aggressive foot with extraordinary activity; but nothing could assuage the pain. Almost mad with increasing torment, I mounted my horse and galloped *ventre à terre* back to Freetown, where in less than two minutes after my arrival I stripped off my trowsers to battle with my bitter little enemies, but so firmly had they buried their forceps in the flesh, that they allowed their heads to be separated from their bodies rather than let go their hold. My legs were really in a deplorable pickle; many hours elapsed before my sufferings were abated, and a considerable degree of fever was the consequence of my meddling with ants' affairs. An instructive lesson, that, however insignificant and contemptible opponents may be, it is an unwise measure gratuitously and unnecessarily to draw upon ourselves their hostility.

The destructive powers of the white ant are beyond credibility: in a house I visited at Freetown, a parrot in a wooden cage was destroyed by them in the course of a few hours during the night. Houses are frequently destroyed by these insects hollowing out the beams and wood-work, leaving them a mere shell, when the superincumbent brick and masonry, losing their support, tumble in; and all this is performed in so short a space of time that there is no arresting the work of destruction. Charring the ends of the beams is the only sure remedy for preventing the evil. I have always paid proper respect to the ant species since my adventure with them at Sierra Leone.

I found the descendants of the Maroons who were transported from Jamaica decidedly the best-informed of the black part of the inhabitants of this pestilential place. A few of the original disturbers of that colony were still alive: among them was one who had made himself a conspicuous character; he styled himself General Montague. The old man appeared to be particularly proud of his rank: he wore an old tarnished gold-laced hat, and something that in days of yore might have been yclept an uniform; from its then tattered condition it could only be a matter of guess-work. He visited me one day at the dinner-hour: it was customary to hand the General a glass of wine upon such occasions; he received the one I presented to him with the air of a man of quality. I endeavoured to glean from him some account of his former exploits, but his memory was treacherous, and his ideas so vague and undefined, that I could elicit nothing of interest or importance: all that can be safely reported is that the wonders he performed excited equally the astonishment of whites and blacks. Obi, or three-fingered Jack, was quite a secondary character to this hero.

Fruit is in abundance at Sierra Leone: pine-apples are as plentiful as blackberries in England, and are delicately flavoured; they may be gathered by the road-side. The tops thrown carelessly away take root during the rainy season and flourish. While lying here, I never saw an alligator, nor did we catch a single shark: if these sea-tigers and disgusting reptiles are plentiful, they were extremely polite to our dog Boatswain, who could not be restrained from indulging occasionally in his favourite element.

A few days previous to our arrival a slave-brig had been brought in by an English merchant vessel under peculiar and painful circumstances. A *prima facie* case was certainly made out from the papers found on board of her, that the owners of the vessel and projectors of the voyage were English subjects; but a link was wanting in the legal chain of evidence to convict them of the misdemeanour, and I believe they got clear off.

This vessel had taken four hundred slaves on board at the Bonny River. Three weeks after her departure, the unhappy creatures had risen upon their oppressors, and murdered the master and the greater part of the crew. Two or three of the latter escaped into the cabin, whence they got into the boat astern, and, cutting away the tackles, were left to make their own way upon the waters: they were never heard of, and doubtless perished.

The ignorant men who had now gained the vessel knew not what to do; not one of them understood the use of the rudder, or the management of the sails. For three months they had been drifted about the ocean at the mercy of the winds and waves. Starvation, thirst, and madness, had reduced these unfortunate beings to about fifty sufferers, when the English merchantman fell in with her. The scene her decks presented is too wretched a picture of human misery to describe; the survivors were in so deplorable a state of exhaustion that it was pitiable to behold them. The master of the merchant vessel did all that humanity could suggest upon the occasion; he quitted his destined course to bring her in, and it was felt to be a hard case by the legal captors themselves, that the vessel he had brought in should be a good prize to the first man-of-war he fell in with, (a brig,) then lying in the river, whose boat boarded both vessels as they entered the port. Such are the laws; it is to be hoped, however, that he was not only compensated for his loss of time and trouble, but that he received a handsome recompense for his meritorious and humane conduct.

I observed that *lusus naturæ*, a white negress, at Sierra Leone. She was the wife of an European tailor. With all the characteristics of the African, her hair and skin were white, but of so singular a hue, that to look upon her created a feeling nearly allied to disgust: to add to the singularity, her children were mulattoes.

The English schooner we had detained at Porto Praya, and one of the Spanish ships, were released by the Slave Court on their paying all the expenses. The Gerona, and Nostra Senhora de los Dolores, with all her slaves, were condemned: the latter vessel was immediately sold, but only part of the cargo of the former was disposed of, it being determined that we should take her to Lisbon. Among the released captives belonging to the schooner was a very fine boy about six years of age. I took a great fancy to him, and, by permission of the Slave Court, I had him bound to me for eight years, hoping I might in after-times ensure a good servant to myself. I brought him home, had him christened, and sent to school, and in due time promoted him to the post of valet. I had every reason to believe the lad was deeply attached to me; but an unconquerable propensity to violate the eighth commandment on every favourable occasion, obliged me to part with him. At the conclusion of the war, I placed him in a West Indiaman, hoping that time would correct his evil fancies; after eighteen months' absence from me, I received so excellent a character of him from the master of the ship, that I was again induced to take him. At the end of two years' further trial, my patience became exhausted; I could not eradicate the passion — it was engrafted in his very nature, and sometimes appeared to be involuntary on his part. Until within a week of quitting my protection, his depredations had been confined to my own property; but, finding he appropriated to himself other people's goods and chattels, I again despatched him to sea.

Sierra Leone abounds in parrots. A sailor belonging to the Tigress had a very fine young bird, which promised so fairly, that I tempted him to let me have it for three guineas, many times exceeding the value of parrots in that colony. Polly turned out one of the best and most amusing of her species; she very early gave a promise of her future fame. She was remarkably good-tempered, and her amiability procured her the run of the gun-room. Poll's incessant chattering sometimes annoyed me; to escape her noisy exclamations, and consequent interruption of my studies, I always popped her into her cage, wrapping a cloak around it; the saucy bird one day set to work, gnawed away one of the wooden bars of the cage, and, making her way through the cloak, perched herself unperceived on the sill of the small window looking into the gun-room.

A black man belonging to the Admiralty Court came on board with the silver oar to take one of the crew on shore as a witness in a cause then pending; he was ushered down into the gun-room, to explain the object of his visit to me. I was at a loss to comprehend his broken English, and exclaimed, "What is that? what do you say, eh?" Blacky repeated his errand. The poor fellow was as much astounded as I was, when, at the conclusion of the message, Polly, with the same voice, emphasis, and pauses I had used, called out, "What's that, eh? what do you say?" From this time Poll was courted, and her talents duly prized — she was a source of real amusement to all my messmates; few days passed on our passage homewards that the captain's compliments were not delivered to the first lieutenant, requesting the honour of Miss Polly's company in the cabin.

She would repeat distinctly anything that was said to her; she called all the gun-room officers by their names, would imitate the noises of the goats, poultry, &c.; and so inimitably did she perform the different intonations of the boatswain's pipe, that a serious accident might have occurred by Polly's piping "Let go!" when a cask of spirits was ascending the hatchway; nor would it have been the first mishap of a similar nature. On such occasions it was found necessary to remove her out of the way.

She would ask so prettily at dinner to be remembered, that she was generally the first served; and when the cloth was removed, she glided from one to the other, sipping their wine, of which she was so immoderately fond, that I have frequently seen her unable to stand, and, lying on her back, roll from side to side, joining in the bursts of laughter she had herself created. It mattered not at what hour of the night I descended to my cabin, I was always welcomed by Poll with a whistle, and "Oh oh, Jem S——, is that you?" If any one attempted to rap her over the bill, she would hold herself back, and scream out, " Ah, ah! will you—will you?" The bird appeared absolutely endowed with sense. I was fool enough to give dear Polly away, greatly to the annoyance of my messmates and the whole of the ship's company: it was an act of injustice to all hands.

The Thais arrived, and we were ready to depart, but a boat from the Arethusa frigate bringing intelligence that she had got on shore near the Isles de Los, we were ordered off with the Tigress to her assistance. In making our way along the coast, we experienced two or three severe tornadoes: the only plan to be adopted by which mischief may be prevented on these occasions is to furl all your sails the moment it falls calm and the heavens threaten a change. To the experienced mariner, generally, there is not much danger to be apprehended from these severe gusts, as the signs that precede them are sufficiently defined to give ample warning.

We found the Arethusa at anchor, making a great deal of water from the serious injury she had sustained. When all had been done that was possible to stop the leak, we proceeded in company with her to Sierra Leone, where Captain Coffin succeeded in repairing the damage so far as to render it safe for her to proceed to England. The greater part of our ship's company were employed in assisting her in this fatiguing duty. It was a day of rejoicing when the temporary repairs of the Arethusa were completed; it assured our departure from this sickly spot. Ere that took place, another governor arrived, only to increase the long list of mortality of his deceased predecessors.

It was determined that the Myrtle should keep company with the frigate, and we sailed with her and our prize the Gerona. A sad accident occurred on board the latter vessel, whilst lying-to for us outside the port scaling her guns: a marine standing in the ship's channels ramming the cartridge home of a gun, the vent of which had not been stopped, it exploded, blowing the unfortunate man overboard, and depriving him at the same time of sight and both his arms. The Gerona had no boat on board except her launch; observing something was wrong, we instantly despatched assistance to her. Before the boat could arrive, the man had been twenty minutes in the water, and, notwithstanding his mutilated state, contrived to keep himself on the surface: an extraordinary instance of human exertion under the circumstances of the case. The poor fellow was brought on board, and heroically bore the amputation of both stumps, but in that climate little hope could be entertained of his recovery: gangrene soon made its appearance, and four days after the accident his sufferings were terminated.

The following day Captain Coffin sent one of his cutters with an officer and crew on board the Myrtle, ordering us to touch at the Gambia for the purpose of again exploring that river in search of slavers, and to rejoin him at Goree. On my second trip up I was less successful. I landed at the town off which I had captured the schooner, and was met by the American agent, who resided there for the express purpose of obtaining cargoes for the slave-ships. He was extremely civil, escorted me over the assemblage of mud huts that constituted the town, and introduced me to the head man of the place, who was also the chief trafficker in his own species. I did not anticipate a very warm welcome from one whose trade it was our duty to destroy. I was not mistaken in my suspicions. I found the old black pursy rogue reclining on a kind of sofa: he was prepared for my appearance, for the moment I came within hail of him he began in his broken English,—

" Wha' for you go fightee blacky marne? Go war wid Bonnyparte: no comee here."

I tried to explain to him the duties of my situation, but his wrath was not to be appeased by my eloquence, and, imagining the old fellow might work himself into a humour for indulging his dislike to the British navy upon my person, I took the earliest opportunity of wishing him good morning. In the apartment I observed three small English iron chests, one of which he opened, filled with gold dust, giving me to understand I had injured him to that amount. It was rather an impolitic step on his part, (after having shown his teeth,) for, had we been so inclined, there was nothing to prevent us, with the force under my orders, from returning during the night and transferring himself and his riches to the boats: a retribution he had richly earned, had it been possible to transport him for the same purpose to one of those spots to which he had sent off so many of his countrymen.

We again bivouacked on James's Island. The rainy season and the heat had doubtless drawn forth the noxious vapours, so destructive to European constitutions; for, before we again reached the ship, several of the people were taken ill: fortunately, we were soon upon the open sea, and the malady was confined to those who had accompanied me, but nearly half of them fell victims to the disease.

The Gambia, I should say, must at all times be prejudicial to Europeans. The low land in its neighbourhood, its muddy shores shrouded with mangrove bushes, the mass of rank vegetation, of which an immense quantity is always in a state of decay, and the forests of wood around, engender in that tropical climate clouds of poisonous miasma; but in the rainy season there issues forth, from every foot of ground, wreaths of pestilence sufficient to sweep off any numbers that may land on its destroying shores. The fever did not terminate in so rapid a decline of the vital powers as in the West Indies; it was of a lingering nature; three weeks or a month elapsed before the last sufferer succumbed to its fatal influence. It certainly was not infectious, for only the men I have already mentioned were attacked by it: a certain proof that the disease was local.

We arrived at Goree, and, receiving no tidings of the Arethusa, correctly supposed that she had pushed on for England, and continued our course.

While on the coast, a native came on board in a canoe, with some of his brethren, and took such a fancy to the ship that he intimated a great desire to remain. Being a strong, able-bodied fellow, well adapted for hauling on board the main tack, we shipped the gentleman as a landsman. He did not speak a word of English when he joined us; all we cauld make out was, that his name was Jumbo, and he was so entered on the ship's books. Jumbo was (contrary to the general character of his countrymen) a hard-working industrious man, possessing great mildness of temper, and an earnest anxiety to make himself useful. With such qualifications he became a general favourite, and the negro-like broken dialect he began to acquire, was a source of great amusement to his shipmates. Any breach of the usual etiquette of a man-of-war was in Jumbo's case passed over, and, from his utter ignorance, he was allowed a latitude which in other circumstances would not have been tolerated; he was much noticed by the officers.

I was highly amused one day at observing Mr. Jumbo leaning with his elbows on one of the quarter-deck guns, supporting his head, and eyeing me with fixed attention and astonishment. I was lying on my back, my head resting on a cushion, sextant in hand, taking the distance between the sun and moon. I was so absorbed with my own occupation, that I did not at first notice blacky; nor did the simple-minded being attempt to interrupt me; but when I had completed my observations, and was consigning the instrument to its case, Jumbo approached.

"Misser Cott, wha' fo' you go lookee sunnee moon, and say top?"*

* It is perhaps necessary for such of my readers as are unacquainted with nautical astronomy to state, that generally four

I carelessly answered, "For them to tell me where we are, Jumbo." An emphatic "Ah!" was the only reply; but, before I left the deck to work the lunars, he sheered up alongside of me.

"Misser Cott, you tellee me sunnee moon tellee you; now pose he tellee you, when Jumbo see de land?"

At this time we had been nearly four weeks from the coast, having been becalmed between Cape de Verd and the islands of that name.— I replied, "Perhaps to-morrow; but come to me by-and-by, and I will tell you."

The longitude deduced from the sights made us about a hundred and twenty miles distant from St. Michael's, to which place we were bending our course. I had scarcely remounted the deck to report the result of the observations to the

persons are employed in taking the lunar observations: one for measuring the distance between the sun and moon, another to take the altitude of the sun, the third that of the moon, and a fourth to note the time per watch, and write down the different observations. The first observer is the principal, who regulates the others; the moment his instrument brings the two bodies into contact, he calls out stop to his assistants, that their observations may agree in time with his. Jumbo fancied I was calling out to arrest the progress of the luminaries.

captain, when Jumbo, who appeared determined to put my knowledge to the test, immediately assailed me.

"When Jumbo see de land, Misser Cott—when um see de land?"

"Why, if the wind holds, we shall see it to-morrow morning."

"Misser Cott, you no' laughee me."

"No, Jumbo, you will see it to-morrow morning at daylight."

"Me see!" with an incredulous shake of the head; and so ended our colloquy.

The following morning before daylight, while the operation of washing decks was going on, Jumbo came across me.

"What are you doing upon deck, master Blacky? it is not your watch."

"No, Misser Cott, it not my wash; you tellee me Jumbo see de land dis marning; when um see um? me like berry much for see um."

Pointing out the direction in which we expected to discover the island, I told him when it was daylight he would see it. I had found by our run on the log board, we could not be more than twenty to thirty miles off. Fixing himself in the waist netting, my friend patiently waited the approach of day, which already began to mark the eastern horizon. It had hardly dawned when the exclamation of the African—" Me see um! me see um!" attracted my attention; his quick sight had penetrated the early mists of morning long before the outline of the high land of St. Michael's became clearly defined to my view. While taking the bearings of the island, Jumbo made his approach towards me something in the fashion of a spaniel dog. I shall never forget the poor fellow's countenance: fear and respect, I think, were the predominant feelings portrayed: but altogether, it formed so odd a mixture of apprehension, admiration, and wonder, that I can scarcely describe it. Not suspecting at the moment what could cause so singular an emotion in the man, I inquired if he was ill, or what ailed him?

" Misser Cott, you raally more big than Mumbo Jumbo."

I now fully perceived the nature of the conflict in his breast. This high compliment placed me above the imaginary being he regarded as a God in his native woods. I endeavoured to make him comprehend that there was nothing extraordinary in the business; but the impression was then too strong to be weakened by any arguments I could advance of my knowledge not exceeding that of the ordinary class of men.

"Misser Cott, pose sunnee moon peakee you, you berry great man;—Jumbo go in um canoe—um no see de land—one day, two day, tree day—sunnee moon no go tellee Jumbo where um be."

I have since speculated much on the variety of ideas that must have traversed the brain of this unsophisticated being; and when the circumstances of the case are duly considered, he may stand excused for attributing to me the gift of supernatural knowledge.

END OF THE SECOND VOLUME.

LONDON:
PRINTED BY SAMUEL BENTLEY,
Dorset Street, Fleet Street.

Printed in Great Britain
by Amazon.co.uk, Ltd.,
Marston Gate.